DISCOVERERS AND ADVENTURERS

R. J. UNSTEAD

ILLUSTRATED BY RON STENBERG

A. & C. BLACK
LONDON

MEN AND WOMEN IN HISTORY

1. HEROES AND SAINTS
2. PRINCES AND REBELS
3. DISCOVERERS AND ADVENTURERS
4. GREAT LEADERS

Also by R. J. Unstead

LOOKING AT HISTORY

PEOPLE IN HISTORY

LOOKING AT ANCIENT HISTORY

A HISTORY OF BRITAIN

THE STORY OF BRITAIN

TRAVEL BY ROAD

HOUSES

MONASTERIES

CASTLES

EARLY TIMES

TEACHING HISTORY
IN THE JUNIOR SCHOOL

LIVING IN A CASTLE

LIVING IN A CRUSADER LAND

LIVING IN A MEDIEVAL CITY

LIVING IN A MEDIEVAL VILLAGE

4, 5 & 6 SOHO SQUARE LONDON W.1

REPRINTED 1967, 1974

ISBN 0 7136 0149 3

PRINTED AND BOUND IN GREAT BRITAIN BY
REDWOOD BURN LIMITED, TROWBRIDGE AND ESHER

CONTENTS

NO VVS
ORBIS

John and Sebastian Cabot

IN the year 1493 a piece of exciting news spread through the seaports and capitals of Europe. A Genoese adventurer named Christopher Columbus had reached the Indies by sailing westwards across the Atlantic Ocean.

No one doubted that the new islands were part of Asia. They were sure to be rich in spices and gold and, since Columbus was in the pay of the King of Spain, their wealth would belong to Spain. The Portuguese, too, were growing rich. Their sailors had made voyages into the Atlantic and along the coast of Africa where, it was said, the rivers ran with gold.

No discoveries had been made by English seamen. So far, they had done little more than sail their fishing-boats to Iceland.

Living at Bristol, however, with his wife and three sons, was a black-bearded foreigner who knew more about the oceans than most men. He was Giovanni Caboto, otherwise John Cabot, a citizen of Venice who, like Columbus, had been born in Genoa.

Like Columbus, too, Cabot was a man with an idea. For years he had wandered from city to city, trying to interest people in a new way to reach the spice-lands of the East. The world, he said, was round. He showed people a globe made of metal; he produced charts and maps to prove that it was easier and quicker to reach the East by sailing *west*.

"When I was a young man trading between Damascus and Mecca," he would tell the Bristol merchants, "I often saw the spice-caravans arrive from the East. The camels were half-dead from weariness, the men were burnt black from crossing the hot deserts. Months, even years, it took them to reach the markets where I bought spices for my masters of Venice. Now, see for yourselves, on this globe. Since the distance by land is so great, the distance by sea must be shorter."

King Henry VII needed money badly. He envied his fellow-monarchs of Spain and Portugal who would soon have gold by the shipload and he wished that he could send out sea-captains to discover new lands.

The King and his Court visited Bristol where John Cabot was invited to explain his ideas for a voyage of exploration. Without delay, Henry VII agreed to provide a ship and he gave Cabot a royal letter, sealed with the Great Seal. It granted "to our well-beloved John Cabot, citizen of Venice, to Lewis, Sebastian and Sanctius, sons of the said John . . . leave and power to sail to all ports, countries and seas of the East, of the West and of the North, under our banners and ensigns . . .".

In 1497 Cabot sailed from Bristol in a ship called the *Mathew*. It was so small that the crew numbered only eighteen men and we do not know if John's sons went with their father. Perhaps they did, for Lewis and Sanctius were never heard of again and they may have died at sea or have been washed overboard. In later years, Sebastian used to say that he went on the voyage. He even spoke as if he, not his father, had

"Land Ho!"

been the captain. But Sebastian was probably no more than fourteen or fifteen years old at the time and he was not always careful about telling the truth.

The *Mathew* left Ireland behind and sailed out into the Atlantic.

"Our course is due west now," said John to the helmsman. "Keep the North Star on your right hand."

Long, anxious weeks went by before the look-out at the masthead shouted "Land-ho!". There on the horizon lay the "new-found land", a bleak headland that Cabot named Prima Vista—first view. In his opinion, he had reached the northerly tip of Asia and he had only to sail on to come to Cathay where he would find the sun-lit cities and measureless riches described by Marco Polo.

It was not China that Cabot had reached, but North America, probably Cape Breton Island. He sailed along the coasts of Newfoundland and Labrador and he went ashore to claim the territory for King Henry VII. In all probability, he set foot on the American mainland before Columbus.

The country was silent and empty. There was no sign of people or houses. The sailors found some snares for trapping animals and a few bone needles that were used, they thought, for making nets, but if there were any inhabitants in the area, they stayed hidden. Cabot was puzzled but not downhearted. He had proved that he was right and, with a larger ship, he could go on to find the Spice Islands. Meanwhile, he would return home to report the discovery of a new land.

If the country lacked riches, the sea was teeming with fish. The sailors had only to let down a basket to have it filled with cod—"England will have no more need of the old trade with Iceland," they cried.

The Mathew *reaches the icy seas of Labrador*

When the *Mathew* reached Bristol, the King was sufficiently pleased with Cabot to give him £10. This seems a very mean reward but in those days it was quite a large sum of money and Henry soon followed it up with a pension of £20 a year. Meanwhile, he gave orders to prepare a bigger expedition.

In May 1498 John Cabot left Bristol on his second voyage. This time he commanded a fleet of five or six ships, one provided by the King and the others by Bristol and London merchants, with local captains on board. Again, we cannot be certain that his son Sebastian was with him.

"I shall follow the coast of the new-found land until I come opposite Cipango (Japan)," John told the ambassador of Milan. "From there, I shall sail straight to the country of the Great Khan and trade with his subjects for spices and silks."

Once more Cabot reached North America and sailed hopefully along the coast, expecting to find a strait that would lead him into warmer seas. Foiled by ice and probably by the fears of his sailors, he had to turn back. For several weeks he coasted down the eastern shore of America, far enough to alarm the Spaniards. He found no gold or spices but he made the name of Cabot renowned among mariners.

The strange thing is that we do not know when John returned home or what happened when he reported that he had found neither treasure nor the way to Cathay. Perhaps the merchants were so disappointed that they cold-shouldered John. Until recently, people believed that he perished in the northern seas but we know now that he was still alive in 1499, for he drew his £20 pension in that

Sebastian impresses the Bristol merchants

year. It seems certain that he died soon afterwards.

By this time his son Sebastian was well known in Bristol. Pleasant, energetic and charming, he impressed people by his knowledge of geography and navigation. He was here, there and everywhere. He visited Spain and France, he knew important people and all about the latest discoveries. He often hinted that he himself had taken part in these adventures and there was hardly anyone who doubted a young man so knowing and clever as Sebastian Cabot.

It was not surprising that the King should award him a pension of £10—not for any voyages, but "for diligent services in and about our town and port of Bristol".

In 1509 Sebastian sailed to Labrador with two ships fitted out at the King's order. He pushed north until he came to a strait leading to the west. Presently, it broadened out and turned southwards. Surely the strait was the North-West Passage and this broad sea was the Pacific Ocean? Cathay must lie ahead.

But the sea was thick with floating ice and, as the perils increased, the sailors mutinied and Sebastian was forced to turn back. Like his father, he sailed along the coast examining every inlet in case it should prove to be a channel leading to the cherished spice-lands. Having thus explored a large part of the North American coast, Sebastian came safely home to Bristol.

At least, that was his story. It seems to be true but no one has ever found a single English document that

The seamen compel Sebastian to turn back

mentions this voyage. The foreigners who wrote about it had heard of it from Sebastian himself!

By this time, Henry VII was dead and, since young Henry VIII showed no interest in voyages of discovery, Sebastian left England and entered the service of the King of Spain. At once he was an important person. He lived at Court where the King made him Pilot-Major of Spain, with a handsome salary and splendid apartments.

Every Spanish captain had to report to the Pilot-Major when he came home from an ocean voyage and no expedition was undertaken without Sebastian Cabot's advice. He examined captains in navigation, gave them their licences to sail, kept records of voyages and supervised the making of maps and charts.

The Pilot-Major of Spain became so celebrated that Henry VIII and Wolsey asked him to return to England to lead an expedition to the North-West. At this, the London merchants protested, saying that "the said Cabot was an impostor, well-known as such, without any real knowledge of the North-West countries, though a glib reciter of other men's tales".

Back in Spain, Sebastian remained in high favour. The King had complete faith in him and nothing could be more natural than to give him command of a great expedition to the Moluccas—the Spice Islands, far away in the Pacific Ocean.

The learned navigator proved to be a complete failure as a commander. After wasting three years in disastrous attempts to find gold in South America, he came back to Spain to stand trial for disobeying orders and for losing his ships and men. Found guilty, he had just been sentenced to banishment in Morocco, when the King of Spain returned from abroad and gave him a complete pardon.

Restored to the post of Pilot-Major, Sebastian remained in the royal service for many years, though he seemed always to have a secret desire to return to England. At length, when he was approaching the age of seventy, the invitation arrived.

The ministers of the boy-king, Edward VI, had decided that they must do something to stir the unadventurous spirits of English mariners. They paid £100 to a ship's captain, Master Peckham, "for the transporting of one Cabot, a pilot, to come out of Hispain to serve and inhabit in England".

As soon as Sebastian arrived, he was given a salary of £166 13s. 4d. "for good services done and to be done" and, from time to time, there were special gifts of £200, doubtless to keep him happy. It was well known that the King of Spain was trying to tempt his celebrated Pilot-Major back to Seville.

But Sebastian was happy in England. The unkind remarks of the London merchants had been forgotten and, among people who knew so little about the oceans, who could doubt the wisdom of Cabot? He was a most jovial old fellow and he entered into his new duties with the utmost goodwill.

England's trade was poor and new markets were needed. Very well, he would speedily put things right. Unfortunately, the Spaniards and the Portuguese had divided the New World between themselves and the way to the East was barred—except by the North-West Passage, and that was both difficult and dangerous. Why not try the North-East Passage and sail to India and Cathay that way?

Sebastian dances at the Christopher

Thus, as Governor of the Merchant Adventurers, Sebastian was "chief setter-forth" of the voyage. He was too old to go himself but he drew up a long list of instructions for Willoughby and Chancellor, the commanders, who set off from Greenwich in 1553.

They found that there was no sea-route to India, only icy seas and a vast frozen land-mass. Willoughby died, frozen to death with his crew, but Chancellor made his way overland to Moscow and he came home with a treaty of trade signed by the Czar, Ivan the Terrible.

English spirits rose. Here at last was a new market for hardware and woollen cloth. The Muscovy Company was formed and its white-bearded Governor went down to Gravesend in high spirits to speed the departure of a new expedition.

The captain of the *Searchthrift* wrote in his journal, "The right worshipful Sebastian Cabot came aboard our pinnace, with many gentlemen and gentlewomen who, after they had viewed our ship, went ashore and the good old gentleman gave most liberal alms to the poor to pray for our good fortune. At the sign of the *Christopher*, he and his friends feasted and made me and my ship's company great cheer. And, for very joy, he entered into the dance with the young people, which, being ended, he and his friends departed, commending us to Almighty God."

So, at the end of his long and rather mysterious life, "the good old gentleman" played his part in awakening Englishmen to the opportunities for trade and adventure across the seas.

Lady Jane Grey

"AND if my Lady will stand still for but one minute, all shall be finished," said Mistress Ellen, as she tried to fasten the little girl's head-dress so that it stood out like a halo round the fair head of the Marquess of Dorset's daughter.

Jane laughed and stopped twisting her head to read her book. The nurse smoothed the bell-shaped overskirt and Lady Jane was ready to make her morning visit to her parents.

She walked sedately across Bradgate's great hall and entered the winter parlour where her parents were seated by the carved fireplace. Jane curtsied and said:

"Right reverend and worshipful parents, I bid you good morning and I beseech you of your blessing."

Henry Grey, Marquess of Dorset, answered briefly, but his wife, Lady Frances, eyed the child coldly and began to chide. Jane's curtsey was ill-done. She mumbled her words. What of her lessons? Was her Greek as far advanced as her cousin's? Had not Master Harding rebuked her for playing too long on the lute?

Lady Frances ended by giving her seven-year-old daughter a sharp blow between the shoulders: "Get you to your lessons," she snapped.

As soon as she left the parlour, Jane's meek expression changed. She hurried eagerly along to the schoolroom where Doctor Harding was waiting. She loved her lessons and could read Latin with ease already. Now she was beginning to learn Greek, French, Spanish and Hebrew.

Between her eighth and ninth birthdays, Jane was sent away from home to live with Queen Katherine Parr, Henry VIII's last wife. Happy with her books and music, Jane knew little of the happenings in the royal household. Henry VIII died and the new king was her cousin, Edward VI, a boy of her own age with whom she often played. Like Jane, he was clever but he was much too young to control the nobles who surrounded the throne.

One of these was Lord Seymour, the High Admiral, a bold, handsome man whose charm so attracted Katherine Parr that she married him within a few months of the old King's death.

The Admiral smiled jovially at the little girl in his wife's household. He went to have a quiet talk with her father.

"She shall be placed in marriage much to your liking," said the Admiral.

"With whom shall you match her?" asked Dorset craftily.

"Why, she might be wife to any Prince. Should His Majesty, when he comes of age, be minded to marry within the realm . . . But, my Lord Marquess, to make so great a match, I must needs have the Lady Jane in my keeping."

For £2000, Dorset gave Jane into the Admiral's care so that he might arrange to marry her to King Edward. But Katherine Parr died suddenly at Gloucester and, soon afterwards, the Admiral's folly brought about his ruin. After his execution, poor little Jane was sent home to her parents. The disappointment made her mother more sharp-tempered than ever.

One day, Master Ascham, Princess Elizabeth's tutor, happened to visit Bradgate. The servants said that all the family were out hunting and only the Lady Jane was at home.

Ascham walked into the house and found the thirteen-year-old girl reading Greek, "with as much delight as if it were a merry story".

"Why, Madam, are you not in the park with the others?" he asked.

"All their sport is only a shadow of the pleasure I find in Plato," answered Jane with a smile.

"But, tell me, how is it you take such delight in books that few men can read with ease?"

"I will tell you," said Jane. "God gave me such severe parents and so gentle a schoolmaster. When I am with my parents, all that I do is wrong and I am so cruelly punished with pinches, nips and blows that I think myself in hell. But when I go to Master Aylmer, he teacheth me so gently that I am happy all the time that I am with him. So you see why books are my pleasure."

Ascham had a long conversation with Jane and, later, he encouraged her to write regularly in Latin and Greek to scholars in England and Switzerland. They wrote back as if to an equal and they found

Master Ascham finds Lady Jane reading Greek

that, like themselves, Jane believed passionately in the new religion of the Protestants.

While Jane was writing to her learned friends, a struggle for power was going on among the lords of the Council. The cleverest of these treacherous men was John Dudley, Duke of Northumberland, who planned to overthrow Protector Somerset.

Having won the young King's admiration—he was a great archer and the best jouster in England—Northumberland made himself all-powerful. Edward and the Council stood in dread of this dark ruthless man who was the real ruler of England. He dominated everyone and he laid his plans to raise his family still higher—as high as the throne itself.

If Edward should die, the heir to the throne was Princess Mary and, after her, Princess Elizabeth. Lady Jane's mother, now Duchess of Suffolk, was next in succession. She was made to give up her rights to her daughter and Northumberland arranged that Jane should marry his son, Guilford Dudley. If anything should happen to Edward VI, it might be possible to see that the crown came to the Dudleys.

So far, Edward seemed to be healthy. He worked hard at his books and he enjoyed outdoor sports. In 1552, however, he caught measles and, although he recovered, he seemed always to be tired. By summer, he was seriously ill.

The Duke increased his hold on the sick boy's mind. Day after day, he spent long hours talking to him about State affairs, voyages of discovery and, above all, religion, for Edward was an ardent Protestant.

In April 1553, Northumberland announced the betrothal of Lady Jane Grey and his son. Jane herself had been told nothing. She hardly knew Guilford Dudley and she liked him less. Elegant and handsome like all his family, he was a conceited booby, a mother's spoilt darling.

"I will not marry Lord Dudley," she said.

The Suffolks stormed at her and struck her until

Northumberland bullies King Edward into altering his will

her spirit was subdued. On 25th May, Jane was married to Guilford Dudley in London.

But the King was dying and Northumberland had to work fast. He spoke continuously to Edward about the succession, working on the boy's fears, wheedling, threatening. If Princess Mary came to the throne, the Protestant religion would be crushed . . .

"But, by my father's will, Lady Mary stands next to me," said the King.

"Where God's glory is in peril, a good prince will set aside a son, a brother or a sister. Think, Sire, of your immortal soul, if you do not do God's Will."

"What then of my sister Elizabeth? She is of the Reformed Church."

"Your Highness does well to ask. If you put aside one, you must put aside the other. Their births were not legal. It is not God's purpose for them to reign."

At last, Edward gave way. Too ill to argue any more, he agreed to leave the crown to his cousin, Lady Jane Grey.

Three judges were summoned to the royal bedchamber to witness the King's will.

"It is not legal," quavered the Lord Chief Justice. He was taken outside to receive the full flood of Northumberland's anger. Next day, the judges returned with the Privy Council to Greenwich Palace where the dying King ordered them to sign. Weeping, they did as they were told and so did a hundred of the chief officials of the realm. Eight days later, Edward VI died.

Meanwhile, Northumberland invited Princess Mary to London. But, as she was setting out, an unknown man stepped forward to whisper an urgent warning. Mary turned her horse and rode away to Framlingham Castle in Suffolk.

Cursing himself for not having seized Mary earlier, Northumberland summoned the Council to attend Lady Jane Grey at Syon House.

On 9th July 1553 Jane entered the great room and was bewildered at being led to a dais under a canopy. She had no idea of the reason for this gathering, for Northumberland had kept the King's death a secret.

With sonorous words, the Duke announced the death of King Edward VI. Jane felt sorrow for the boy whom she had once known so well . . . but what was the Duke saying? The Lady Mary . . . the Lady Elizabeth . . . disinherited—what could he mean?

"His late Majesty hath named your Grace as heir

to the crown of England. Therefore, you should cheerfully take upon you the name, title and estates of Queen of England, France and Ireland!"

Queen of England? In terror, Jane saw that the lords were kneeling. She tried to speak, to run away. Almost fainting, she cried through her sobs:

"No! No! The crown is not my right. The Lady Mary is the rightful heir!"

The Duke and Guilford Dudley tried to calm her. Her parents lost all dignity and ranted at the white-faced girl until she fell upon her knees and begged God to tell her what to do. There was no answer and she took the silence to mean that she must obey. She rose and the lords came forward, one by one, to kiss her hand. She was Queen of England.

Next day, to the boom of cannons and the harsh blare of trumpets, Jane entered the Tower of London in state. She was so small that she was made to wear clogs with three-inch soles, but she held herself like a monarch, smiling prettily, as she walked from the Water Gate on the arm of her gorgeously decked husband. She was too excited to hear the vintner's boy cry:

"The Lady Mary hath a better title!"

In the royal apartments of the Tower, they brought Jane the crown and the jewels, but it was some time before she would allow the Lord Treasurer to try the crown on her head.

"Another shall be made for your husband," he said. Jane looked up. Now she realized why Northumberland had made her Queen—so that a Dudley should be King!

"No," she said firmly, "that cannot be. I would be

The Lords of the Council kiss the hand of Lady Jane

content to make my husband a duke. But I will never consent to make him King."

"I *will* be King!" cried the spoilt youth, bursting into tears. In the furious storm that broke over her head, Jane remained calm. When Guilford's mother declared that she would take her son home, the fifteen-year-old Queen said quietly:

"He shall not leave. His place is here and, whether he likes it or no, he shall remain."

Two days passed without trouble from the Londoners, but Northumberland's sons were routed when they took a force into East Anglia to capture Princess Mary. At this, the Duke decided to send Jane's father, the Duke of Suffolk, but once again Jane was obstinate.

"My father shall stay here in my company," she said. Because he dared trust no one else, Northumberland rode angrily out of London at the head of his army. By the time he reached Newmarket, there was news that men were up in arms for Mary. His troops began to desert and, at Cambridge, the Duke panicked.

Seeing that the game was up, he tore down the notices proclaiming Lady Jane and shouted, "Long live Queen Mary!". Nothing could wipe out his treason and Northumberland was arrested and brought to the Tower through a crowd of jeering Londoners.

Nine days after the Council had knelt to kiss Jane's hand, Suffolk hurried to the room where Jane was at supper:

"Daughter," he said, "I am here to tell you that you are no longer Queen. You must put off your royal robes and be content with a private life."

Northumberland on his way to the Tower

"I shall put them off more willingly than I put them on," replied Jane. "I did so out of obedience to you and my mother, but I sinned and I gladly relinquish the crown."

Then she added piteously:

"May I not go home?"

But Suffolk had already gone. To save his own neck, he sneaked out of the Tower to add his voice to those who shouted for Queen Mary.

Placed under arrest, Jane was moved to a small house on Tower Green where the Gentleman-Gaoler looked after important prisoners. Her husband was in another part of the Tower and she saw nothing of him or her parents. However, her attendants were kind, she had her prayer-book and she wrote a long letter to Queen Mary, confessing that she was wrong to have accepted the crown.

She learned that, although she and her husband would have to stand trial for treason, the Queen would not allow her to die.

There was no pardon for Northumberland. He went to the block in grovelling misery, admitting that he had even betrayed his religion and was never at heart a Protestant. Jane watched from her window as he went to his death:

"I pray God," she said scornfully, "I nor no friend of mine die so miserably."

Six months passed. Jane wrote letters and prayers, while Guilford occupied himself with carving his family arms on his prison wall. They had stood their trial and both were under sentence of death, but they fully expected to be pardoned.

From time to time, news filtered into their prison. Queen Mary was determined to marry Philip of Spain and the people were angry. There were riots in the City; Catholic priests had been stoned and there was talk of rebellion.

In Kent, Sir Thomas Wyatt led an armed rising that was meant to be a protest against the Spanish marriage, but Jane's father foolishly joined in. The affair was bungled and Wyatt was captured at Temple Bar. Two days later, Jane was told to prepare herself for death.

"Master executioner, I forgive you for what you have to do."

Mary was not a harsh woman and she had no wish to end her cousin's life. But, whispered her advisers, as long as Jane Grey lived, there would be plots and rebellions. The Queen sent a priest to see if the girl would become a Catholic; that alone might save her.

Jane was young and she did not want to die:

"I am innocent and I do not deserve this sentence," she said. "Lord and Saviour, suffer me not to be tempted above my power."

Her Protestant religion meant more to her than life and, although she liked the priest and kissed him farewell at the end, she did not yield.

On 12th February 1554, at ten o'clock in the morning, she caught a glimpse of her fair-haired husband as he passed beneath her window on his way to Tower Hill. Shortly afterwards, still watching, she saw the cart return with his headless body. She closed her eyes for a moment, picked up her prayer-book and went downstairs into the open air.

The scaffold was on the Green and she walked towards it, a tiny figure in black, holding the Lieutenant's arm. She was quite calm, "her countenance nothing abashed, neither her eyes moisted with tears".

She spoke briefly to the spectators and forgave the executioner. Without assistance, she tied the handkerchief about her eyes. Then she stretched out her arms, crying:

"Where? What shall I do?"

Someone guided her towards the block and she knelt down. The people heard a clear, girlish voice cry out:

"Lord, into thy hands I commend my spirit."

John Hawkins of Plymouth

WHEN Queen Elizabeth came to the throne, a young sea-captain was trading out of Plymouth. He was John Hawkins, younger son of William Hawkins, a leading merchant of the town.

John and his brother William were partners in the family business but, so far, the warehouses and the shipyard held no attraction for John. He preferred to go to sea and had already made several voyages to Spain and the Canaries where his fair dealing and his ability to speak Spanish made him popular with the local gentry.

At this time, England and Spain were allies and Queen Elizabeth was anxious to keep on good terms with Philip of Spain.

Thus, for a young man with a good knowledge of the Spanish trade, there might be opportunities to increase his business. John Hawkins left Plymouth and went to London, taking with him £10,000, his share of the family fortune. Soon he married Katherine, daughter of Benjamin Gonson, Treasurer of the Navy, and was introduced to some gentlemen of the Court and of the City. They were interested in taking shares in a trading venture and they asked about his plans:

"Sirs, I intend to sail to the Gold Coast," said Hawkins.

"Doubtless to trade for gold, ivory and spices like your father?" remarked Sir Thomas Lodge.

"No, sir," replied Hawkins. "The Portuguese make great difficulty in that trade. I have in mind to buy negroes to sell them to the King of Spain's subjects in America."

"But doth not His Majesty forbid all trading by foreigners in those waters?"

"It is true, sir, that a licence is required. But I have friends in Spain who can ease such matters. The plain fact is that the planters need negroes most urgently and will pay handsomely for them."

In the 16th century no one saw anything wrong in buying and selling slaves. The trade was well established and King Philip levied a tax on each negro sold to his settlers. Even so, slaves were scarce and expensive in the Spanish colonies.

In 1562 Hawkins sailed to West Africa with four ships. By capture and by purchase from Portuguese traders, Hawkins collected 400 negroes and set sail for the West Indies. At Hispaniola, the Spanish

Hawkins and the Spanish officials

governor and officials were surprised to hear themselves addressed courteously in Spanish.

"Honoured and excellent sirs," began Hawkins, "I am come to offer you merchandise at fair prices. You may assure yourselves that I intend no harm to you or to the interest of the King's Majesty of Spain whose servant I am."

The officials were taken aback. They ought not to trade with a foreigner, but this Englishman was richly dressed and well spoken—perhaps he had powerful friends in Spain. A little trading in a quiet place along the coast could do no harm—and they would tell Captain Bernaldez to conceal some soldiers in hope of taking the stranger unawares.

But Hawkins was too wily to walk into a trap. He met Bernaldez in the open, with his own men close behind, fingering their weapons. The Spaniards smiled and bowed. The trading was completed with goodwill on both sides and the Englishmen sailed for home, satisfied with their profit.

In London, the success of this first voyage led to preparations for a bigger expedition. This time, the Queen provided one of her own ships, the *Jesus of Lübeck*. It was an old vessel, leaky and difficult to handle, but Hawkins felt honoured to sail in her as his flag-ship, and even more honoured to be summoned to the Queen's residence at Enfield.

If Elizabeth had expected to meet a bluff Devon sea-dog, she was disappointed. The captain was as elegant as any gentleman of her Court in his fashionably padded doublet of black velvet, with cuffs and collar of fine cambric. But it was his charm and eager loyalty that impressed her most. As for Hawkins, for the rest of his life he was to see Elizabeth as she was then—still young and handsome, with the dazzling air of majesty that entranced her poets, statesmen and mariners.

On his second voyage, Hawkins again collected slaves in West Africa and crossed the Atlantic to the Spanish Main. By a mixture of charm and veiled threats, he again sold his goods and negroes at a good profit. Then, after giving generous assistance to a distressed French settlement at Florida, he returned to England and thankfully brought his leaky old flag-ship into Padstow.

From his cabin he wrote to the Queen, "Thanks be to God, our voyage is reasonably well accomplished".

The Plymouth captain was now in high favour with everyone, except the Spanish Ambassador who wrote privately to his master, King Philip.

Elizabeth receives John Hawkins at Enfield

"I saw him at the palace and invited him to dine with me. The vast profit of his voyage has excited other merchants and Hawkins is going out again next May . . . I might tell the Queen he has traded in ports forbidden by Your Majesty and ask her to punish him . . ."

Elizabeth refused to punish her famous captain but, to avoid a quarrel, she would not let him sail in the following year.

For once, Hawkins may not have minded. There were business affairs with his brother in Plymouth and his own son Richard was now five years old. The boy was big enough to trot after his father through warehouses, into a ship's hold and upon the poop-deck where he could play at being a sea-captain and could learn from his father how things should be corded, stowed and made ship-shape on a Hawkins vessel.

Meanwhile, there was a good deal of mystery about the preparations for the third voyage. Stories went about that Hawkins had agreed to serve King Philip in the Mediterranean, that two Portuguese runaways were going to lead him to a gold-mine in Africa and that a Spanish admiral tried to stop his ships leaving harbour.

However, in October 1567, Hawkins left Plymouth with six ships—the *Jesus*, the *Minion* and four small vessels supplied by the Hawkins family, including the *Judith*, soon to be commanded by their nephew, young Francis Drake.

It was more difficult than ever to collect slaves in West Africa. Nor were things any easier in the West Indies and along the Main. Stern warnings from Spain had made the planters unwilling to buy and, in one place, Hawkins had to capture the town in order to do business. However, almost everything was sold and, with a great sum in gold, pearls and silver stowed aboard the *Jesus*, it was time to go home.

Almost at once, the little fleet ran into a hurricane. The *Jesus* was leaking so badly that she could hardly be kept afloat and, at all costs, Hawkins had to find a haven where he could make repairs.

In the Gulf of Mexico, he came to San Juan de Ulua. Flying the faded royal standard instead of the Cross of St. George, he was able to slip past the fort that guarded the harbour-mouth because the Spaniards mistook his ships for a Spanish plate-fleet, expected at any time.

Hawkins made himself clear to the astonished Governor:

"I desire only to repair my ships. I will pay for

Hawkins and the Governor of San Juan de Ulua
"I desire only to repair my ships!"

victuals and I will not take a pennyworth of your silver or gold."

The Spaniards made no difficulty and work began at once.

Next morning, a lookout sighted the Spanish fleet approaching. What was to be done? Hawkins had taken the fort and his guns were ready, so it would be possible to keep the fleet out. But that would be an act of war.

"There is no help for it," he said to Drake. "Our two countries are at peace. I must let them in and trust to the Spaniards' honour."

Both sides promised not to molest the other but, as soon as his fleet was inside, Don Martin, the newly arrived Viceroy of Mexico, prepared for action. Two days later, in a sudden attack, the men working ashore were massacred, and Spanish guns opened fire on the English ships at their moorings.

Hawkins ran on deck to see that the *Minion*, alongside, was being boarded. "God and St. George!" he roared, "Upon the traitorous villains!" Leaping down, he drove off the attackers and turned to repel a similar assault on the *Jesus*.

"Cut the head cables!" he ordered. "Haul off into the harbour."

Clear of surrounding craft and, having told Drake to take the *Judith* outside, he attacked the Spaniards so fiercely that two of their galleons were sunk and the rest silenced. But the shore batteries continued to pour shot after shot into the *Jesus* until she was in a pitiable state. Hawkins therefore used her to shield the *Minion* while the gold and silver were transferred

The gold and silver were transferred into the smaller ship

into the smaller ship. This work was not quite finished when two fireships came blazing towards them.

Frantically, the men cut the *Minion* free and, as the ships parted, Hawkins was the last to leap to safety. By tremendous efforts, they got out of the harbour and anchored for the night near to the *Judith*.

Next morning, for some reason never explained, Drake had vanished, leaving his commander in the lurch. Hawkins, who never liked to blame an officer, merely reported later that "in the night, the *Judith* forsook us to our great misery".

They were indeed in misery. The *Minion*, badly damaged, had two hundred men on board and very little food and water. It would have been suicide to try to sail home, so a hundred seamen volunteered to be put ashore along the coast in hope of surviving until help could arrive from England.

It was a nightmare voyage for the others. Only fifteen men were alive when they sighted Devon and they were too weak to bring their ship into Plymouth. A relief crew was sent out and, from the rail, a gaunt figure thanked them. Dressed in his finest clothes and wearing a gold chain, John Hawkins came bravely into his home port.

He found that Drake had already arrived and all England was buzzing with the story of the treachery at San Juan. From this time on, no matter what Elizabeth and Philip pretended, there was unofficial war with Spain.

At home with Katherine and young Richard, Hawkins soon recovered his strength. By summer, he was at sea again, this time commanding a fleet that helped the Dutch and French Protestants in the Channel. But he constantly put his own plan to the Queen's advisers.

"With God's grace and a good squadron at the Azores," he told the Earl of Leicester, "I can take the King of Spain's treasure-fleet and avenge the wrongs done to this realm."

The Queen gave him permission to fit out ten warships at Plymouth but she always found reasons to prevent his sailing. The truth was that she needed her wily captain at home and Hawkins became Treasurer of the Navy, guardian of all the royal ships. Faithfully, tirelessly, he toiled to create the kind of Navy that he knew was needed, bringing the old-fashioned ships up to date, rebuilding half-decayed galleons, introducing more powerful guns and better pay for the seamen.

Instead of going to sea as he longed to do, he found himself dealing with shipwrights and timber merchants, with the fitting-out of fleets for other commanders, and he saw his nephew Drake take his own place as England's most celebrated sea-captain.

For his great work, he earned hatred and suspicion. By putting a stop to the dishonest practice of over-charging the Queen for timber, ropes, canvas and every kind of naval stores, he made enemies in high places. They accused him of "cunning and craftiness to maintain his ambition and pride and for the filling of his own purse".

In fact, Hawkins grew poorer, not richer, in the Queen's service, but he stuck to his task:

"The true test of my work will be seen when Her Majesty's ships meet the Spaniards," he said.

Hawkins in the Shipyards

In 1584 Hawkins managed to get to sea but he was only allowed "to ply up and down the Channel and guard the coast" instead of going to intercept the treasure-fleet as he hoped. However, he was pleased that his new ships handled so well and when, four years later, the Armada came sailing up the Channel, they did not fail.

Hawkins commanded one of the four squadrons that dogged the Armada like terriers and finally broke its formation. Thanks to their seaworthiness, their guns and the luck of the weather, they saved England from invasion.

With the danger past and the kingdom frantic with joy, Hawkins, who had been knighted on the Lord Admiral's flag-ship, was still hard at work. Off the coast of Kent and in the seafaring towns, he was trying to cope with thousands of sick and starving sailors for whom there was little food and no pay. Somehow, he got the survivors back to their homes but he never forgot the plight of those seamen.

In later years, he and Drake founded the Chatham Chest, a fund to help distressed mariners, and he also built the Sir John Hawkins Hospital for old seamen and shipwrights.

By this time Hawkins was going on for sixty. He was tired and he wished to resign from the Navy to go back to Plymouth where his brother and his wife had died and his son Richard was now a sea-captain in his own right. But the war with Spain continued and the Queen would not release him, so he continued to serve her for the rest of his life.

He built some fine new ships but he grieved at the waste of money on unsuccessful land operations. For

half the cost, he could have taken a fleet to sea to cut off the King of Spain from his Empire and his gold.

The Queen grew ever more obstinate and tight-fisted, so that even Drake was half in disgrace and Hawkins was constantly in trouble over the expenses of the Navy.

Perhaps this was why the two ageing sea-captains put forward a plan to rob the Spaniards in the old style. Permission was given and in 1595 they sailed from Plymouth as joint-commanders of a powerful fleet.

It was a disastrous expedition. The two men, never close friends since San Juan, were entirely different—Hawkins, thorough and methodical, Drake, fiery and

The fight at Porto Rico

impatient of another's ideas. They did not quarrel openly but there was no harmony and the Spaniards, better armed and stronger than ever, had already learnt of their coming.

At Porto Rico, the English met so fierce a reception that even Drake's genius could not prevail, and by this time Sir John Hawkins was dead. On the day before the attack, he had died on board the *Garland* and his last thoughts were for the Queen. "Assure Her Majesty," he murmured, "of my love and loyalty." Since he was not able to bring her the treasure that he had intended, he left her £2000 to make amends.

In his own ship and serving his Queen to the end, Hawkins died as he had lived, a loyal Englishman.

Sir Philip Sidney

"THIS child may save us yet from all our perils," said Sir Henry Sidney, looking fondly at his new-born son.

His wife, Lady Mary, smiled a little sadly.

"I pray God that he may do so," she replied. "Then he will be the first of my luckless family to aid my husband."

Lady Mary was the daughter of John Dudley, Duke of Northumberland. Barely a year had passed since her father's execution for treason. Her brother, Guilford Dudley, had gone to the block on the same day as Lady Jane Grey, and four other brothers were still in the Tower.

Yet Queen Mary was not a vengeful woman and she sent Sir Henry Sidney to Spain to escort King Philip to England. Two weeks later, Sir Henry rode into the courtyard of Penshurst Place, his grey manor-house in Kent. He dismounted and ran to his wife's room:

"Great news!" he cried. "The King himself is coming to our child's naming!"

So, in December 1554, at a magnificent christening ceremony, King Philip of Spain was godfather to an English baby. Naturally, the child was named Philip in his honour.

While little Philip Sidney and his sister were learning to walk and to explore the rooms and gardens of Penshurst, their father was away in

Philip and Fulke Greville at school

Ireland, trying to subdue the rebels. Just before Philip's fourth birthday, Queen Elizabeth came to the throne and at once showed that she had not forgotten that the Dudleys were her childhood friends.

Lady Mary was called to Court. Her brilliantly handsome brother, Robert Dudley, became Earl of Leicester, the Queen's favourite, and Sir Henry Sidney was made Lord Deputy of Ireland and Lord President of Wales.

Philip went to Shrewsbury School, not far from Ludlow. A boy called Fulke Greville started there on the same day and they became friends for the rest of their lives. Both were good at lessons and at the school sports of tennis, archery and running. Philip was more serious than his friend but he was so friendly and generous that all the boys seem to have looked upon him as their leader.

After four years at Shrewsbury the two friends went up to Oxford, and in the long holidays there were visits to Ireland and to the magnificent London home of Philip's uncle, the Earl of Leicester. Sometimes he stayed at the home of William Cecil, the Queen's minister. Cecil was very fond of his friend's son and wrote to Sir Henry:

"Your Philip is here; he is a boy worthy to be loved and so do I love him as he were mine own son."

In 1572 Philip obtained the Queen's permission to travel abroad. Walsingham, the English Ambassador in Paris, gave him a cordial welcome and introduced him to Catherine de Medici, the Queen Mother. This terrifying woman smiled graciously upon the nephew of the great Earl of Leicester, for she was hoping to marry one of her sons to Queen Elizabeth.

Meanwhile, tremendous preparations were afoot for the marriage of Catherine's daughter to Henry of Navarre and Paris was thronged with people who had come to attend the royal wedding.

During the night of 24th August, St. Bartholomew's Eve, Philip was awakened by screams and the clash of weapons. Hundreds of French Protestants were being dragged from their beds to be butchered in the streets. As a foreigner, Philip was safe in the English Embassy but, as an ardent Protestant, he was horrified by the massacre.

"If the Protestant countries do not bind themselves into an alliance," he cried to Walsingham, "they and their religion will be overthrown."

"Softly, Philip, it is not wise to speak such thoughts aloud," replied the Ambassador. "For the love I

St. Bartholomew's Eve

bear your parents, I would have you leave Paris at once. An escort will ride with you to Frankfurt."

After Philip had made his farewells to the Walsinghams and their pretty daughter, he departed to Germany and continued his travels into Italy.

People were enchanted by the slim young Englishman. Princes, merchants and scholars welcomed him into their homes. He studied languages and science and talked to learned men about politics and religion. He became an expert fencer and, under the tuition of the Emperor's riding-master, a brilliant horseman.

At last, the Grand Tour came to an end and Philip went home to Penshurst to see his parents and his admiring young brothers. He was nearly twenty-one and eager to begin his career as a statesman. Mary, his favourite sister, was already a maid-of-honour at Court and it was not long before Leicester, his uncle, introduced Philip into the circle of elegant young men who attended the Queen.

Her Majesty was about to set out on one of her progresses through part of the kingdom. Her sharp, green eyes looked approvingly at Leicester's nephew and she gave him a jewelled hand to kiss. "I do require you to accompany our progress," she murmured.

By October, the Court returned to London and Philip went to live at Leicester House. Sea-captains and soldiers of fortune came in and out, with talk of voyages and alliances, but, for a young man thirsting for adventure, there was strangely little to do.

Philip hated idleness and he obtained permission to assist his father to rule Ireland. Often, he carried despatches to the Queen and one day, to his delight, she chose him to go abroad as her representative.

It was an important mission for a young diplomat. He travelled to Prague to greet the new Emperor and he had also to find out how things stood in Europe. Philip needed all his charm when he called, first, upon the Spanish Viceroy of the Netherlands and then upon William the Silent, leader of the Dutch.

After his return, Philip was sure that the Queen would find some splendid task for him to carry out. It might be a voyage, an armed expedition, the founding of a colony . . .

"And it please Your Grace," he suggested eagerly, "I would raise a company to aid our friends in the Netherlands against their oppressors . . ."

The Queen smiled and asked him to arrange a hunting-party for the morrow.

"Within a month, Master Frobisher doth sail to the New World. I beg leave of Your Majesty to accompany him."

Elizabeth changed the subject. No matter what Philip suggested, she always found a reason to keep him at Court. It seemed as if she could not bear to let him out of her sight. Rather than lose him, she wasted his brilliant talents.

One day, Philip protested so hotly about this boring existence that the Queen rebuked him angrily.

Feeling himself out of favour, he went down to Wilton, the lovely home of his sister Mary, now Countess of Pembroke.

Mary and her brother had remained close friends since their childhood. Both loved books, poetry and the countryside. Both were clever and high-spirited, but this summer Mary was unwell and Philip was bored.

To amuse his sister and to pass the time, Philip began to write a long story-poem.

"This is my joyful book," he told Mary. "It is to be full of quaint things, all written as prettily as your most flowery poet. It will magic away our melancholy."

"This is my joyful book."

Set down on odd bits of paper and passed laughingly, a page at a time, to Mary, the poem was never finished. Years later, as he lay dying, Philip remembered his "joyful book". It had been written carelessly for fun and he asked his friends to burn it. They could not bear to do so but had it published with the title *Arcadia*.

The Queen restored Philip to favour. He had just been knighted when he heard that Drake and Frobisher were preparing an expedition to the West Indies. Eagerly, he offered to take part.

It was secretly arranged that Drake should command the fleet and that Sir Philip Sidney should lead the land forces.

When all was ready, Philip and Fulke Greville rode down to Plymouth. To their dismay, Drake refused to sail unless they had the Queen's permission and he insisted on writing to London to inform Her Majesty of the gentlemen's intention.

"There is but one thing to do," said Philip to his friend. "I will post my men outside the town to seize the Court messenger. If the letter is not to our liking, we will send it back!"

The Queen was furious when she heard of this defiance. She sent for a peer of the realm and ordered him to bring Sir Philip Sidney back. If he did not come, he would be banished for ever.

"Tell him," she added softly to the royal messenger, "that I have other work for him to do."

Six weeks after Drake sailed, Philip was made Governor of Flushing, the Dutch sea-port. He was also to be second in command of an English army that was about to leave for Holland under the Earl of Leicester. William the Silent had been murdered and it seemed as if the Spaniards were about to overrun the country.

Sidney found the defences of Flushing in a poor state and most of the soldiers were sick and ill-armed. He put new heart into the garrison and sent to Leicester, urging him not to delay in England.

The attack on Axel

Unfortunately, when Leicester arrived, he seemed more interested in banquets and costly ceremonies than in fighting the Spaniards. Little was done in the winter of 1585, and when spring came the Dutch situation was desperate. The Spaniards, under their brilliant general, the Duke of Parma, were pressing across the country towards the coast. If the seaports fell, all was lost.

Sidney and Count Maurice, William the Silent's valiant son, felt that they must act. To distract the Spaniards, Maurice asked Sidney to lead an attack on the town of Axel.

With a thousand men, Philip left Flushing by night and rowed up the Scheldt for twenty miles. He joined forces with Maurice and the allies marched through the darkness towards Axel.

Near the town they halted. With forty picked men, Philip went ahead until the moat was reached. In the darkness, he and his men slipped quietly into the water, pushing ladders as they swam. They scaled the gates, overpowered the sentries and opened the gates to their comrades before the defending garrison realized what had happened.

This exploit revived the spirits of the Dutch people and Leicester began to show signs of his old energy. He moved his headquarters to Arnhem and agreed to attack the nearby towns of Doesburg and Zutphen.

The smaller town, Doesburg, was captured by assault, with Sir Philip leading a storming party that included his brother Robert and the young Earl of Essex.

Realizing that the allies would attack Zutphen next, Parma despatched a convoy with food and ammunition to enable the garrison to hold out. Hearing of this plan from a prisoner, Leicester sent five hundred men to ambush the convoy, but he did not know that it was accompanied by a powerful escort.

Very early in the morning, Sidney and a number of cavalry officers left camp to inspect the ambush-party. Despite a thick mist, they found the men well positioned on a hillock near to a church.

As they prepared for action, Sidney noticed that two of his brother-officers were not wearing thigh-pieces because of recent wounds. Not wishing to go into battle better armed than his friends, he threw aside his own leg-armour.

The rumble of waggons and the clatter of men and horses could be heard. Suddenly the mist lifted.

There, below the knoll, was the convoy moving towards Zutphen with its heavy escort of pikemen, musketeers and cavalry.

Outnumbered six to one, the Englishmen charged. A series of savage hand-to-hand encounters took place. The English withdrew, formed up and charged again and then a third time.

In the second charge, Sidney's horse was killed. Flinging himself upon another animal, he dashed in again and cut right through the enemy. As he wheeled, a musketeer fired at him from short range. The ball struck his unguarded thigh, smashing the bone. His terrified horse plunged wildly, but when a trooper came up and offered to lead him to the rear, Sidney waved the man away.

"Look to yourself, let them not see I am wounded," he said.

He got the horse under control and rode in agony back to his uncle's camp. Seeing that he was badly hurt, men ran to aid him: he asked for water and a bottle was brought. As he raised it to his lips, a soldier, fearfully wounded in the same engagement, was carried by. Sidney saw the dying man's eye light up with longing and he handed the bottle to him.

"Thy necessity is yet greater than mine," he said. Leicester was appalled by his nephew's appearance:

"Oh, Philip!" he cried, "I am truly grieved to see thy hurt."

"My lord," answered Sidney, "this have I done to do you honour and Her Majesty some service."

They took him by barge to Arnhem where he lay for twenty-five days in the house of a Dutch widow. His young wife, Walsingham's daughter, was brought

Sir Philip at Zutphen

from Flushing to nurse him, his brothers came whenever they could leave the war; Leicester was constantly at his bedside and the Queen wrote a comforting letter and ordered the messenger to return immediately with news of his health.

For a time, it seemed as if he might recover. He was so calm and cheerful that his friends did not suspect the terrible condition of his wound. The surgeons had been unable to reach the musket-ball and, though he joked with them, composed verses and set them to music, he knew that his life and all his hopes were ended.

On 17th October 1586, scarcely thirty-two years old, Sir Philip Sidney died at Arnhem.

Protestant Europe mourned him. Philip of Spain when he received the news in a despatch wrote at the bottom of the page, "He was my god-son".

In England, people felt that they had lost the brightest and noblest of their young men. They gave him the stateliest funeral that ever filled the streets of London and his father-in-law Walsingham ruined himself to pay for it.

Thirty years later, his friend Fulke Greville asked that no words should be written on his own tomb, except:

"Fulke Greville,

Counsellor to King James I. Servant to Queen Elizabeth" and then, the highest honour that he had ever known,

"Friend to Sir Philip Sidney".

Captain John Smith

MASTER George Mettham looked severely at the tousled, sunburnt boy who stood in front of him:

"Thou are a grief to me," he said mournfully. "Thy father, God rest his soul, entrusted me to keep thee at thy books and afterwards to put thee to farm his land. But I find that all thy days are taken up with horse-riding, wrestling and sword-play. Hast thou no wish to be a farmer?"

"Sir, my mind is set upon the sea," replied the lad.

"I feared as much," continued his guardian, "but I would make more of thee than a common sailor. Therefore I have spoken to Master Sendall, ship-merchant of Lynn, and he will take thee as apprentice. Tomorrow, we shall ride to Lynn."

John Smith left his Lincolnshire village with a light heart. He was sixteen, a strong unruly lad, determined to see the world and to make a name for himself.

But King's Lynn was a sorry disappointment.

Instead of going to sea, John found that his master set him to work in a warehouse. This was no life for an adventurer so, one day, he threw down his pen, packed his clothes into a bundle and set out on foot to London.

In time, he reached France where he worked for a while as a nobleman's servant and then he enlisted in a company that was leaving to fight in the Low Countries.

"In the two years that I served the Dutch," said John afterwards, "I learned to ride a horse in battle, to use lance, musket and axe. But I had no taste for killing fellow-Christians, so I took my pay and made for home."

In 1599 he was back at Willoughby in Lincolnshire. His gruff guardian had managed the farm well and there was money to fit himself out like a gentleman, so John purchased some first-class weapons, several suits, shoes, books and a couple of iron-bound chests to pack them in. He was ready for anything that offered travel and adventure.

At this time, the Turks were pressing into eastern Europe and when John learned that the Emperor was raising an army to defend his territory, he decided to set out for Vienna to enlist as a soldier of fortune.

On the way, he fell in with three rascals who stole his chests containing all his money and clothes. However, he reached Marseilles and managed to obtain a passage to Italy. After a series of adventures, including a spell as gunnery officer on board a French pirate ship, he came to Vienna and joined the Imperial Army as a soldier of artillery.

John Smith and the Turkish champions

In the war against the Turks, the young Englishman soon gained a reputation for bravery and cunning. Promoted to the rank of captain, he entered the service of Prince Sigismund whom he greatly admired. During the siege of a town called Regall, Captain Smith became the most renowned soldier in the army when he killed three Turkish champions, one after another, in single combat. For this feat, he was awarded a pension of three hundred ducats and the right to wear on his shield-of-arms the three Turks' heads.

The Christians pressed the enemy back but one of

their armies, advancing too rashly, became trapped in a valley by a horde of Tartars.

Some of the cavalry escaped but the rest of the army was slaughtered by the half-savage tribesmen. Next day, some Tartar soldiers were stripping the bodies of the dead, when they came across Captain Smith, lying fearfully wounded among the slain. Noticing that he was still breathing, they carried him to their camp and tended his wounds in order to sell him in the slave-market.

John soon recovered, only to find that he had been bought by a Turkish noble who sent him in chains to Constantinople as a gift to the Lady Tragabizanda, a maiden to whom this nobleman was betrothed.

The young lady took an interest in the handsome slave and she was talking to him one day when her mother chanced to come into the courtyard. Horrified to find her daughter conversing with an infidel, the old lady declared that she would get rid of him at once. At this, the fair Tragabizanda sent John to her brother who was the Pasha or Governor of a distant province.

Fettered to a servant, John arrived in Cambia in southern Russia. The Pasha, having heard from his mother, had decided to punish the Christian for daring to speak to a high-born Turkish maiden. John was beaten unconscious, an iron ring was riveted round his neck and, presently, he was put to the hardest tasks on the estates.

One day, he was alone threshing corn in an outlying barn when the Pasha came by and began to revile him and to beat him with a heavy riding-whip. John defended himself and, in a terrible struggle,

Smith's escape

killed his persecutor. Quickly, he threw off his rags and put on some of the dead man's garments. He filled a sack with corn and, mounting the Pasha's horse, galloped away into the open plains.

For days, he rode in a north-westerly direction, not daring to approach the occasional encampment that he sighted on those vast grasslands. At length, he came to a broad track that was used by trading caravans and this led him to a town on the Russian frontier. The Governor received him kindly, provided him with food and lodging and sent him on to the next town.

Across Russia and Poland, John travelled from city to city until he reached Leipzig in Germany. To his surprise, he found that his old lord, Prince Sigismund, was living there in exile. The Prince gave him his discharge from the army, with 1500 ducats in gold and a document granting him a coat-of-arms.

"It is right that you should return to your own country after suffering so many hurts in my service," he said. "Do not forget, brave captain, to wear the three Turks' heads for ever."

In 1605 Captain John Smith came home to England. He had been away for five years and his career as a soldier of fortune was ended.

* * *

With James I on the throne, war with Spain was ended and all the talk in London was of colonies and settlements in North America.

In a tavern, John was talking to Captain Gosnold who had recently returned from America.

"This land named Virginia is a goodly land," said Gosnold. "It hath great forests and broad meadows. The Indians are few in number and appear to be a kind, loving people."

"Then surely this will support many Englishmen who have no work to do?" cried Smith. "With God's help, you and I shall plant a settlement in Virginia!"

Men, ships and stores were needed. John Smith and Gosnold found a number of gentlemen willing to put money into the venture; the London Virginia Company was founded and in December 1606, three ships were ready to sail with 150 pioneers on board.

Commanding the ships was Captain Newport.

The leaders of the expedition were Captain Gosnold, Master Wingfield, Captain Archer and Ratcliffe.

From the start, Smith was unpopular. The ne'er-do-wells and down-at-heel gentlemen disliked his plain speaking, for he made no secret of the fact that he despised their laziness.

Smith in irons during the voyage to Virginia

"This fellow means to make himself captain over us all," complained his enemies. Despite Gosnold's protests, they had Smith put into irons for most of the voyage. Indeed, some wanted to hang him then and there.

On arrival in Virginia, the Company's orders were unsealed and it was found that Captain Smith was named as one of the seven Councillors appointed to rule the colony. Naturally, he had to be set free and, to his enemies' relief, he merely laughed in their faces and said:

"I do not doubt, gentlemen, that ye will show as much zeal with spade and axe as ye did in locking me up!"

The ships anchored in Chesapeake Bay and a landing-party went ashore to choose a place for the first settlement, called James Town, in honour of the King. While they were examining the countryside, a file of Indians crept unnoticed towards them and let fly a shower of arrows. Two sailors were wounded and, although a volley from the muskets sent the Indians shrieking into the woods, it was clear that the first task must be to protect the settlers. Smith, the experienced soldier, soon had trees felled and hauled into position to make a triangular fort in which he mounted several cannons on platforms of logs and earth.

Meanwhile, the stores were unloaded from the ships and, in June, Captain Newport sailed back to England leaving the colony to fend for itself under Master Wingfield, the first President.

Summer in Virginia was very hot. The river almost dried up and, at low tide, it stank, as did the marshes nearby. Most of the stores were found to be mouldy and, since it was unsafe to go far in search of game, the settlers had to live mainly on fish, crabs and berries. Many of the men fell sick and there was much grumbling, especially by those who had never been used to hard work out of doors. Archer and the grumblers deposed President Wingfield and put Ratcliffe in his place. During these events, Smith and Gosnold were seriously ill. Gosnold died but Smith recovered and helped to nurse the sick.

Building the fort

Ratcliffe proved to be a weak, idle man, and Smith could see that the colony was doomed unless he himself could obtain food. Boldly, he went to the Indians, holding out coloured beads, axes and pins to their fascinated gaze. In exchange, they gave him venison, corn and pumpkins that helped the sick to recover.

"Our troubles are not ended," warned Smith. "How shall we live unless we provide for ourselves? I shall place you in companies, one company to hew trees, another to clear the land and to make it ready for seed. We must have better houses and a church. Let every man take on the hardest task as his own share!"

As winter approached, Smith built up a store of food. He traded with the Indians, learned their language and came to respect their courage and skills. But he did not trust them. He knew that they hated the white men and would wipe them out if it were not for their fear of the muskets.

North America was still unexplored and, whenever he could leave the settlement, Smith would take a party by barge up-river to trade and to increase his knowledge of the country.

On one of his expeditions, he persuaded an Indian, by gift of a copper kettle, to act as a guide. He chose two companions and, having ordered the rest of his company to keep watch and not to leave the barge, he set off into the woods.

Several miles inland, Smith and his Indian guide were walking some distance ahead of his two companions when he heard a ghastly cry behind him. Quickly whipping a cord round the guide's arm to bind him to his own wrist, Smith drew his pistol and turned back, thrusting the man before him as a shield. He found that his friends were already dead and that he himself was surrounded by two hundred Indians. The guide called out that this was the chief of the white men whom they ought to take alive.

Seeing the Indians pause, Smith slipped the cord off his wrist and made a dash for freedom, only to plunge up to his armpits in a swamp. The warriors pulled him out half-dead with cold and dragged him to their village.

He was brought before the Chief, a splendidly built man with an air of majestic dignity, who gazed at the prisoner for a long time. Smith gazed calmly back and then, with the utmost gravity, drew from his jerkin a pocket-compass and solemnly presented it to the Chief. The Indian was fascinated. He and his warriors tried to touch the quivering needle but could not because of the glass. What was this thing? What did it say? John explained the use of a compass. He told them about the stars and the tides, how the earth moved and how the white men had found their way across the great ocean.

The Indians were awe-struck by this wise man who spoke their own language and explained such great mysteries. Food was brought for him and presently he was led to a wigwam and invited to rest there.

After many days, during which John was treated almost like a god, the Indians told him that they were going to take him to their Great Chief.

They set out, travelling across country, and came to the village of Great Chief Powhatan who actually lived only about twelve miles from James Town. His 'palace' was a long barn-like building made of branches covered by bark and John's guards thrust him inside, forcing a way through the dense throng of warriors, squaws and children to an open space at the far end where Powhatan, surrounded by his wives and counsellors, was seated upon a pile of embroidered cushions.

Gravely, the Chief questioned the prisoner. Why had he come to this land? What was the secret of the white man's magic? How did the rods speak with thunder? Smith's answers seemed to please him, for Powhatan ordered dishes of meat and bowls of sweet corn to be brought in, and he invited the prisoner to join him in eating. Growing bold, Smith began to speak of King James, boasting of his cities, his ships and his armies. Powhatan's expression changed to alarm. He turned to his counsellors and, in a moment, two large stones were brought in and placed on the ground. Four men came forward bearing heavy clubs. The white man was to be killed by having his brains dashed out.

All this time, a graceful, dark-eyed girl of about fourteen had been eagerly listening and watching from her place among the royal wives. She was Princess Pocahontas, Powhatan's favourite daughter, and when she saw that the prisoner was condemned to death, her eyes filled with tears of pity. Smith, intending to show that he could die as bravely as any Indian, looked round calmly and then knelt down and placed his head upon the stones. As the clubs were uplifted, Pocahontas darted forward and threw herself beside the Englishman so that the warriors dared not strike.

"Spare him!" cried Pocahontas

"Spare him!" she cried to her father. "Spare the stranger! It is not good to kill so wise a man."

There was silence. As Powhatan recovered from his astonishment, the thought came to him that the girl was right. It would be foolish to kill this man when he might exchange him for gifts that would make him lord over many more tribes.

"Let the white man stand up," he said at last. "I shall have further talk with him tomorrow."

A few days later, on condition that he gave them two cannons from the fort, Captain Smith was escorted to James Town by twelve warriors. He had been away for five weeks and the colony was in a worse plight than ever. All the stores had been eaten and only thirty-eight men were left alive. When they saw their one real leader striding towards the fort between his guards, the settlers rushed out and embraced him.

"We believed you to be dead!" they cried. "How did you survive among the savages?"

"Almighty God and a little Indian maid preserved my life," replied John. "But, first, let me deal with these guards."

He turned to the Indians and took them to see the cannons mounted on their platforms:

"Take them to your Great Chief," he said.

But of course the warriors could not budge the great guns that each weighed more than a ton.

"Ah, I forgot. They have big stones in their mouths," said Smith, smiling. "We must empty them."

He ordered both guns to be fired and the Indians fell terrified to the ground. When they had recovered, they declared that they would much rather take some blue beads to Powhatan and soon they left happily, with beads, hatchets and a special gift for Pocahontas.

As soon as they had gone, Captain Smith began to put the colony in order. He arrested Archer and some of the troublemakers and he summoned the others to a meeting.

"Do not despair," he said. "I have seen much of this land and if we but play our parts like men, we shall prosper yet."

Next day, a party of Indians arrived, carrying great baskets filled with venison and bread. With them was Pocahontas who had come to see the English town and to talk to her brave captain. After he had shown her all the houses and the church he thanked her most courteously and presented her with the prettiest ornaments in his store.

Throughout the winter, the little princess brought many gifts of food to the settlers. She saved their lives and they came to look upon her as an angel sent by Heaven to preserve them.

When spring came, Captain Newport sailed into Chesapeake Bay with a ship-load of stores and a hundred new settlers. Unfortunately, they were another batch of down-at-heel gentlemen, servants, soap-boilers and glass-blowers:

"Twenty good workmen would have been better than them all," growled Smith.

Ratcliffe and Archer were delighted to have fresh allies, for the newcomers were soon grumbling about the bearded captain who never ceased badgering them to sow crops and to stand guard.

"By order of the London Company, we are here to discover gold," they retorted. "Furthermore, it is

Indians caught stealing weapons

well known that you have dealt harshly with the Indians but we are to treat them with gentleness."

In their folly, the new settlers tried to curry favour with the Indians who began to come in and out of the fort as they pleased, stealing hatchets, knives and even muskets.

One day, Smith caught some of them as they were carrying off armfuls of weapons. Promptly, he clapped them in the town jail and when Powhatan sent his warriors to the rescue, they were scattered by the thunderous cannons. To appease the terrible captain, the Indians soon brought back a large number of stolen weapons as well as gifts of food.

Gradually, the colony began to prosper. John Smith's work was recognized at last, when the settlers elected him President in 1608. He had the church rebuilt, the fort strengthened and new storehouses prepared for the harvest. Fresh fields were planted and every Sunday the whole colony was put through their armed drill so that they would be able to defend themselves in time of need.

More settlers arrived in the autumn and, once again, Smith had to teach them that they had come to Virginia to make homes and not to pick easy riches. A few Dutchmen tried to betray the colony by giving arms to the Indians and the settlement had to withstand some fierce attacks as well as the more serious threat of starvation.

Smith was undaunted. He overcame every difficulty, defeating the Indians, sometimes by force and often by cunning. Pocahontas saved his life a second time when she warned him of a surprise night attack and, at length, his stubborn spirit so impressed Chief Powhatan that he made terms and, for as long as Captain Smith remained in Virginia, the English and the Indians lived together in peace.

By 1609 the colony was thriving so well that John began to think of building a new settlement up the river. He was returning to James Town by boat one evening, when he fell asleep resting his head on a bag of gunpowder. One of the men, in lighting his pipe, dropped a spark and the powder exploded. In flames, John leapt overboard and when his men rescued him and lifted him tenderly into the boat, his injuries were so terrible that they believed he was certain to die.

For weeks he lay at James Town more dead than alive, but gradually his strength prevailed and he began to recover. However, he was very weak and his injuries were so severe that he was persuaded to return to England to be treated by skilled doctors.

In October 1609 John Smith left Virginia for ever.

"Alas!" cried his friends, as the ship stood out to sea, "We have lost the man who built this colony and saved all our lives."

* * *

The founder of Virginia recovered his health and, less than three years later, he was commanding an expedition to New England. This was so successful that a Company was formed to establish a colony there but, on his way out as Admiral of New England, Smith was captured by French pirates and his crew came back with the story that he was dead. However, he escaped in a small boat, was wrecked on the coast of Brittany and reached home penniless. Unable to find support for yet another expedition, Smith took up a new way of earning a living. He turned author and settled down to write the story of his travels. In addition, he prepared maps and leaflets about America and these were used by many travellers, including the Pilgrim Fathers.

From time to time, some of his friends from Virginia would call to see him and, one day, to his great delight, two soldiers who had served with him against the Turks turned up at his home to talk over their old adventures and escapes. On another occasion, he actually met Pocahontas who had married an Englishman in Virginia and was visiting London. The little princess was so overcome by the sight of her brave captain that she could not speak at first but could only weep for joy.

Smith did not live to a great age, for he died in 1631 at the age of fifty-one and he was buried in the parish church of Holborn in London.

William Harvey

THE body of a well-built man lay on a table in the anatomy theatre. Tiers of wooden seats, rising one above another in circles, were crowded with students who looked almost straight down at the dissecting-table where neat rows of knives and probes were laid next to the body.

Two college officials entered the theatre, walking side by side with solemn tread. The Clerk followed, carrying a white rod. All the students rose as the great Doctor Fabricius came in and seated himself in a high-backed chair opposite the body. The Masters of the Anatomy, his assistants, positioned themselves at either end of the table with the instruments ready.

With a low bow, the Clerk presented the white rod to the Doctor; the officials withdrew and the Anatomy Lecture began.

Deftly, the assistants opened the body of the criminal who had been executed for robbery a few days previously. They exposed the lungs, heart and liver as their Master directed by pointing with the rod.

During his lecture, Doctor Fabricius did not fail to mention his notable discovery that in the veins of the body there were valves like tiny trap-doors whereas the arteries had no valves at all. As the Doctor proceeded to explain this little-known fact, a student, seated with the Scots and the Englishmen,

The Anatomy Lecture

leaned forward as if anxious to catch every word. Noticing this movement, the old Doctor smiled benevolently for the student was one of the most brilliant pupils he had ever taught.

After one hour, the Demonstration ended and the Clerk cried aloud:

"This lecture, gentlemen, will be continued at five of the clock precisely!"

The white-aproned, white-sleeved Doctor and his assistants left the candle-lit theatre and the students, breaking up into noisy groups, followed them into the bright Italian sunshine.

Deep in thought, the student who had leaned forward so eagerly walked away by himself. He was William Harvey, twenty-two years old, a native of Folkestone in Kent. He was the eldest of seven boys, the "week of sons" born to Thomas Harvey, a prosperous merchant engaged in the Turkey trade.

In the year of the Armada, the merchant had sent William, aged ten, to the King's School at Canterbury and, six years later, to Cambridge. Having gained a good knowledge of Latin and Greek at the university, William went to study medicine and the sciences at Padua, near Venice.

Harvey was still thinking about the lecture when his friends, Fortescue and Darcy, sighted him by the river, gazing thoughtfully at the water.

"Hey, Will! Will, I say, art thou deaf?" hailed Fortescue. " 'Tis dinner-time. If the Doctor had me on the table, he would open an empty belly!"

Harvey laughed and turned to his friends:

"Yet, still I do not see how the blood can ebb to and fro like the sea, as our masters tell us. Does it not flow perhaps, in a stream like this river?"

"It is foolish—aye and dangerous—to question the teaching of centuries, Will," replied Darcy. "Let be and come to thy dinner."

Not long afterwards, Harvey gained his degree as Doctor of Medicine and returned to England. In 1602, he settled in London as a member of the College of Physicians.

Wilmot and Goring, a pair of brave but drunken officers, opposed him at every turn.

"This fire-eating Prince will pillage London as if it were some German town," they warned. "He speaks to no one but only cries "Pish" to gentlemen who were soldiers when he was at his mother's knee."

Ignoring Rupert's plan, Charles made a leisurely march to Oxford and set up his headquarters there before advancing in gingerly fashion towards London.

Rupert raced eagerly ahead, attacking outposts and probing the enemy's defences. His cavaliers sacked the little town of Brentford but, by now, the Parliament-men had recovered their nerve.

At Turnham Green, they stood firm in gardens and orchards where cavalry were useless. They had plenty of ammunition and they would not budge. The King retreated to Oxford.

Hesitation had cost him the war but, for the moment, no one believed it. The Royalists seemed to be successful everywhere and Rupert covered himself in glory as he raked the home counties with the cavalry and organized a ring of strong-points round Oxford.

While the Court settled itself comfortably in the colleges, he was hardly ever out of the saddle. He captured Cirencester, Lichfield and a dozen smaller towns, won a brilliant engagement at Chalgrove Field and joined forces with Prince Maurice outside Bristol. Together, they stormed the defences and captured the great seaport.

Colonel Fiennes, the Parliamentary commander, was granted the honours of war and was permitted to march out of the city with his men. Some of the Royalists began to taunt and plunder them as they passed. Horrified by such behaviour, Rupert and Maurice dashed in among their own men, beating them left and right with the flat of their swords. Having restored discipline, Rupert apologized to Colonel Fiennes and rode with him until he was clear of the crestfallen Royalists.

Soon after the capture of Bristol, Queen Henrietta Maria arrived from abroad with a hundred waggon-loads of stores and weapons. The King's fortunes were at their peak and victory seemed certain.

But, in truth, Charles was far from strong. He could not give the supreme command of his armies to Rupert because of the jealousy of his senior officers. His Court was filled with quarrelsome schemers, money was running out and ammunition was always short. Although Rupert won one engagement after another with the cavalry, the King lacked the infantry to win a war against such men as Fairfax and Cromwell.

By 1644 the Royalist cause was beginning to fail. With Digby, full of bad advice at his elbow, Charles left Oxford and marched about the west country with little purpose. In the north, Lord Newcastle and the last remnants of the King's forces were closely besieged in York.

Rupert was sent to save the situation. Like a whirlwind, he tore through Cheshire, relieving garrisons and capturing towns until he came to Bolton. On foot, he forced his way into the town to win one of the most savage victories of the war. While his soldiers ransacked the houses for food, he took from

Rupert and Maurice beat their own men for plundering the Parliamentarians

his pocket the King's letter. His orders were clear:

"I command and conjure you that, laying all else aside, you immediately march with all your force to the relief of York."

His army was too small for the task but, by a brilliant manoeuvre, he evaded three Parliamentary armies and entered the city.

"He does not always think . . ." wrote Rupert's mother years before. It was still true. The Prince assumed supreme command of all the troops in York without a thought for the feelings of Lord Newcastle, a strange, touchy nobleman who was practically a king in his own northern county.

"You have no choice in the matter, my Lord"

"Tomorrow, we meet the enemy at Marston Moor. Have your men ready to march at dawn," said Rupert curtly.

Newcastle eyed this arrogant youngster in a sweat-stained tunic:

"My troops are worn out from the siege and Your Highness's men would look the better if they were clean and rested. I do not choose to fight tomorrow."

"The King's position demands it," snapped Rupert. "You have no choice in the matter, my Lord."

Next day, Newcastle's men had not arrived when Rupert was positioning his own troops. An officer remarked:

"The enemy outnumber us two to one, sir. Besides my Lord Fairfax and the Scots, they have Cromwell commanding the Horse."

Rupert brightened. He had never met this squire whose skill with cavalry was said to equal his own:

"Is old Ironsides here?" he cried. "Will he fight?"

A Puritan trooper who had just been brought in for questioning, nodded grimly. Rupert turned to the man:

"So he will? Here, my friend, go back and tell the Lieutenant-General that he shall have as much fighting as he likes."

The trooper was released and presently Cromwell's answer came back:

"By God's grace, so shall Prince Rupert!"

Newcastle's whitecoats arrived so late that they had to be stationed at the rear but it was almost dusk and too late for a battle. Rupert gave the order to stand easy and went to his supper. At that moment, Cromwell charged.

The Royalists never recovered. To his horror, Rupert saw his own cavalry fleeing in confusion.

" 'Swounds, do you flee?" he roared. "Follow me!"

He rallied his second line. Goring fought magnificently on the left but the odds were too great. Many of the infantry threw down their arms but the whitecoats refused to fly and died fighting where they stood.

It was night when Rupert came across Lord Newcastle and some officers at York.

"What will you do?" asked one.

"I will go to Holland. I will not endure the laughter of the Court," growled Newcastle.

Prince Rupert spoke briefly:

"I will rally my men."

He went out into the darkness and mounted his horse. He had met defeat for the first time. The King's cause was ruined but he was still a soldier. He would rally his men and he went alone, for Boy, the white poodle, had perished somewhere in the fighting.

By dawn, he had collected together the greater part of the cavalry and, beating off their pursuers, they rode to the Welsh border. As Parliament's army steadily wore down the Royalists, Rupert fought on. He captured Leicester but when the enemy came up with superior forces, he advised the King to retreat. Charles and Digby overruled him.

At Naseby, Rupert beat Ireton's cavalry but Cromwell had sufficient reserves to turn his terrible Ironsides against the King's infantry in the centre. Charles lost his army, his guns, baggage and even his private papers. The end of the war was in sight.

Ordered to hold Bristol with the remnant of the cavalry, Rupert looked at the city's crumbling walls and remarked to Maurice:

"His Majesty has given us a task here, brother."

Sir Thomas Fairfax surrounded Bristol. His troops easily breached its defences and, to prevent the slaughter of the unhappy citizens, Rupert offered to surrender. Fairfax allowed him to march out "with colours, pikes and drums" and, as he courteously accompanied the Prince out of the city-gate, they passed Cromwell, sitting grim and silent on his horse.

The loss of Bristol was a bitter blow. In the agony of defeat, some of the Royalists declared that Rupert had betrayed the cause. Some even whispered that he had surrendered the city for money.

King Charles refused to see him. Instead, he removed him from his command and told him to leave the kingdom.

"I will not submit to such base treatment," cried Rupert. "This is Digby's doing. With the friends we still have, let us go to the King."

Rupert passes Cromwell after the surrender of Bristol

By speed and cunning, he crossed four counties and came to Newark Castle. Without ceremony, he burst into the King's presence, demanding to be heard. Charles continued to eat his supper without so much as looking up.

Four days later, after Rupert had been tried by court-martial, the King signed a document stating that his

"right dear nephew was not guilty of cowardice or disloyalty!"

But the Prince was not restored to his command and, having taken a cold leave of his uncle, he rode away from Newark with Maurice and two hundred gentleman of the cavalry. Charles stood at a window and wept to see them go.

Rupert was deeply hurt but, once he had recovered his temper, he knew that he could not desert the King in the hour of defeat. He swallowed his pride and asked to be pardoned for his ill-mannered conduct. They were together at Oxford when Charles decided to escape in disguise in order to give himself up to the Scots. Rupert begged to be allowed to accompany his uncle.

"Nay, your great height would give us away," replied the King.

With the war ended, Parliament treated Rupert and Maurice generously. They were permitted to leave the country and, in July 1646, the Prince reached St. Germain, near Paris, where Queen Henrietta was keeping up a threadbare Court.

* * *

Rupert received a hero's welcome in France. The boy-king, Louis XIV, made him a Marshal and presented him with command of an army in Flanders. However, he was so severely wounded in the head that he was obliged to return to Paris to recover his health.

One day, word arrived that some of Parliament's sailors had mutinied and had sailed their ships to Holland. With Maurice and Charles, the young Prince of Wales, Rupert went aboard in the hope that they might win over the entire Navy. Once at sea, it was clear that the unpaid seamen were much keener on piracy than on rescuing the King from the Isle of Wight.

In disgust, Rupert returned to Holland. At least, he had nine ships and he resolved to continue the war in his own way.

Sea-outlaws

His mother sold the last of her jewels to equip the little fleet and, in January 1649, Rupert and the ever-faithful Maurice sailed to southern Ireland.

For a time, they cruised about, capturing Parliamentary ships and dividing the booty between their crews and the exiles in France. At Kinsale, they were horrified to hear of the King's execution and startled to find that Admiral Blake, Parliament's great naval commander, was lying in wait for them with a powerful squadron. For three months, they were trapped in harbour until a gale scattered Blake's ships and allowed them to slip across the Bay of Biscay to Portugal.

Blake chased after them and the sea-outlaws had to make for the lawless waters of the Mediterranean where they supported themselves by piracy until Blake's relentless pursuit made them decide to try their luck in the West Indies.

Off the Azores, two ships went down in a storm, one with three hundred men aboard, and Rupert had a narrow escape when transferring to the *Honest Seaman*. The survivors made for the west coast of Africa where they not only obtained meat and fresh water but succeeded in capturing four English vessels. The largest of these, the *Defiance*, became Maurice's flag-ship and, in good heart, the buccaneers again set course for the West Indies.

They were disappointed to find that all the English islands were now in Parliament's hands. However, they cruised about, adding steadily to the plunder below decks until a hurricane scattered the fleet.

When the wind dropped, the ships were terribly battered. The *Honest Seaman* was a total wreck and the *Defiance* had vanished. Dull, faithful Maurice, who had stood by Rupert since childhood and had never once questioned his leadership, was never seen again.

Sorrowfully, Rupert sailed for France in the *Swallow*, the only sound ship that was left. His ill fortune continued to the end, for the *Swallow* went aground and the Prince reached St. Germain with hardly a penny to show for three years' buccaneering in the name of the King.

Once again, he was met with rapturous compliments and Louis XIV sent his own coach to carry the hero through the streets of Paris. Once again, the old jealousies came to the surface as soon as the cheering had died down.

Young Charles II and his courtiers were desperately poor and they had been longing for Rupert to return with shiploads of gold. Where was the money? What had Rupert done with the treasure? Charles II, a debonair spendthrift, half believed rumours that the Prince must be concealing a fortune.

People began to say that Rupert had changed. His old gaiety had turned into a brooding melancholy:

In exile, Rupert returns to his old hobbies

"Prince Rupert goes little abroad," reported one of Parliament's spies, "and is very sad that he can hear nothing of his brother Maurice."

In fact, Rupert was ill. Fever had weakened his great body and the wound in his head caused unbearable pain until it was relieved by opening his skull to remove a piece of metal.

Hurt by the King's attitude and disgusted by the company of men like Digby, Rupert left Paris. He was heard of in Heidelberg, Cologne, Holland, Hungary and Vienna. Rumour had it that he was commanding an army for the Emperor in Eastern Europe.

The truth was that he had returned to his old hobbies of chemistry and drawing. Among his inventions was a method of engraving pictures on metal that is called *mezzotint*, and he was living quietly, in semi-poverty, trying to perfect this process when he learned that Cromwell was dead.

Charles II gained his father's throne in 1660 and he at once invited Rupert to England. On his arrival, he rewarded him with a pension of £6000 and the posts of Vice-Admiral of the Fleet and Governor of Windsor Castle.

As if by magic, Rupert's gloom vanished. At long last, his loyalty was recognized; he had a home and work to do. With all his old zest, he threw himself heart and soul into the business of the Navy and into encouraging merchant ventures, especially the Hudson's Bay Company and the exploration of Canada.

During the Dutch War Rupert commanded a squadron and took part in several sea-battles. His great raid on the Dutch coast when over a hundred enemy vessels were destroyed led to the famous attack on Chatham. The Navy was blamed for this disaster but Rupert, in a towering rage, told the King why the war went badly:

"The fault lies not in His Majesty's officers and men," he bellowed, "but in the horrible neglect of provisions, pay and the work of the shipyards. Damn me if I can thrive at sea until some have been hanged on land!"

As in the old days, his blunt words and fiery temper earned the enmity of some people. But the men adored him, especially when he threatened to take a cane to the Navy Commissioners and when he actually sent a shot through the rigging of a captain who flew the wrong flag! Poor little Mr. Pepys, Clerk to the Navy, trembled in his shoes and wrote spitefully, after a committee meeting:

"Prince Rupert do nothing but swear and laugh a little, with an oath or two and that's all he do."

Even the King stood a little in awe of his fire-eating cousin for he remarked ruefully:

"With the Prince coming here today, I must expect a chiding."

But the fierce old Admiral had a quieter side to his nature. He took delight in showing people the improvements he had made at Windsor, his collection of old weapons, his horses and the splendid hounds in his own pack.

He never married and the Court bored him, so he took himself off to Windsor to his workshops. Besides cannons, firelocks and nautical instruments, he invented a revolver, a new method of boring gun-barrels, a powerful kind of gunpowder and he even experimented with a torpedo and amused himself by forging coins to annoy the Master of the Mint! Some of his finest mezzotints are still at Windsor Castle.

Prince Rupert died in 1682 and was buried in Westminster Abbey. He was the bravest, cleverest and most faithful of all the Stuarts.

William Dampier

ONE morning in the early years of Charles II's reign, a thin dark boy received a thrashing for not having learned his Latin grammar. He was William Dampier, son of a Somerset farmer, and, instead of memorizing Latin verbs, he had been poring over the pages of a book called *Voyages touching the Discovery of America.*

The schoolmaster's stick was heavy. It interrupted a day-dream of distant lands where brilliant birds flashed in the forests and dark men drove canoes along unknown rivers. But it did nothing to weaken the boy's determination to be a traveller.

William's parents died when he was about sixteen, and within a year he had left farming to his older brother George and was sailing to Labrador in the charge of a Weymouth skipper. By the time he was twenty-one, he was a hardened seaman who had voyaged to the East Indies and had seen some hot fighting against the Dutch when serving with Prince Rupert's squadron.

William was at home on sick leave when a local landowner offered him the chance to manage a plantation in Jamaica. He accepted the offer because, as he said:

"I have ever had a thirst for knowledge and experience."

Up country in Jamaica, life was so dull that he

Log-cutting in Campeachy Bay

threw up planting and went down to the waterfront to look for a ship.

He spent a year on a coaster, trading in and out of the lovely islands of the West Indies before joining a band of the toughest ruffians on earth. They were the logwood-cutters of Campeachy Bay and, for two years, Dampier cut and hauled the valuable timber, working in tropical heat, knee-deep in water with his hard-drinking companions.

By this time he was keeping a journal. At night, when his workmates were carousing, he would write up his notes about the strange plants, birds and animals that he had seen:

"The monkeys that are in these parts are the ugliest I ever saw. The fowls are humming-birds, a pretty little feathered creature no bigger than a wasp."

He described things that people at home had never heard of—garr-fish, sea-devils, "tiger cats"—and he noted the difference between alligators and crocodiles, the taste of turtles and cooked snake, the way to plant coconuts and the Indians' methods of making canoes.

When a hurricane swept away all his hard-earned cash and possessions, Dampier was forced to do what many another unlucky man had done. He joined the buccaneers.

His crew-mates included criminals, mutineers, gentlemen-of-fortune and escaped slaves. There was an old soldier who had served under Cromwell, a couple of drunken doctors and a few educated men who had fallen on hard times.

As always, Dampier made the best of the company he was in. He was strong and he did his work with the best. There was something aloof about him, and his dark face and thrust-out underlip warned the roughest cut-throat that he might be a dangerous man to cross.

His first buccaneering was brief and bloody. There was an attack in open boats on a Spanish town where a dozen men were killed but the only loot was a quantity of salt-beef and some red and yellow

At this time, the best-paid and most highly respected medical men were physicians. They were well educated but nearly all their knowledge was based on the teachings of the Ancient Greeks. It was almost a crime to suggest that Aristotle or Galen might ever have made a mistake.

In Harvey's day, the common diseases were leprosy, ague, smallpox, influenza and the "sweating sickness". The remedies for illness were curious. Even the College of Physicians approved such strange medicines as crabs' eyes, buttered live spiders, partridge feathers, baked mice, ants' eggs and powdered human skull!

Harvey bought a house in St. Martin's parish, near Ludgate, and here he brought his bride, Elizabeth, daughter of Launcelot Browne, who had been physician to Queen Elizabeth.

The young Doctor built up a good practice and among his patients were the Lord Chancellor, Sir Francis Bacon, the Lord Treasurer and many of the gentry in the capital.

When he went about London, the Doctor rode in style, with a "foot-cloth" draping his horse almost to the ground, while his servant trotted along behind. Known to everyone as "little Doctor Harvey", his short spry figure, his curly hair, olive complexion and dark eyes, as bright and quick as a bird's, gave him a foreign air. He walked and talked quickly, waved his hands about in conversation and, rather to the alarm of some people, had the habit of playing with a small dagger that he wore at his belt. Although he gave the impression of being a fierce little man, he was really gentle, full of jokes and acts of kindness.

Dr. Harvey in London

As a physician, Harvey dressed soberly in doublet and breeches of a purple-brown colour, with a large turned-down white collar in place of the old-fashioned starched ruff of Elizabeth's reign. Outdoors he put on a long cloak and a broad-brimmed hat, but when lecturing or seeing patients he wore the small black cap of his doctor's degree. On two or three mornings a week, the little doctor would step briskly through the narrow lanes of the City until he came to St. Bartholomew's Hospital. There the Hospitaller would have patients brought to him in a room with a big open fire-place.

Seated at a table, he would gaze intently at each patient on the settle opposite him. Then he felt his pulse, asked him a few questions and prescribed the treatment and medicine for his illness. As always, he made careful notes in a large book that was kept locked when not in use—though his handwriting was so terrible that no one could have read it if he had left it open!

After this, he would go into the wards to see patients who were too ill to be moved. Unlike most physicians, he did not think it beneath his dignity to

Harvey at work in his "museum"

examine patients closely. Far from despising the surgeon's art, he took every opportunity to increase his knowledge of the body and he often performed operations with his friend, Master Woodhall, the leading surgeon of the day.

Each evening, after he and his wife had dined together, in the company of Elizabeth's pet parrot, a fine bird that was a renowned talker, Harvey would retire to a room behind his study. Here, in his "museum", as he called it, he spent all his spare time, dissecting every creature that he could lay hands on—rats, mice, eels, frogs, rabbits, birds and snakes. Their pickled remains filled the jars that stood on shelves round the room. In cages and fish-bowls were dozens of live creatures that he studied.

Sometimes, at night, with only his servant for protection, he would go to a hospital or a prison in order to discover the cause of a person's death. Having opened the stomach or the skull, he would conceal his investigations by skilful sewing and leave for home before daylight.

Harvey pursued this work in secret because, in his search for knowledge, he would have aroused the anger of those who believed it was wicked to question the age-old beliefs. For centuries, men had believed that the blood was produced in the liver and that two kinds of blood, one in the veins and the other in the arteries, moved slowly up and down the body.

In men and animals, Harvey studied the heart; he worked out the amount of blood in the body and he observed the working of the lungs. The old theories seemed to be wrong, but he knew that he must *prove* his own opinions.

He remembered how his old Master at Padua had pointed to those little valves in the veins, but Fabricius had never been able to explain why they were there. After much thought and experiment, Harvey saw the explanation. The valves meant that blood could flow in one direction only and that direction was *towards* the heart. There were not two kinds of blood after all. There was one mass of blood that was pumped by the heart round and round the body "in a kind of circle". The blood, he said, was "cleaned" in the lungs and the arteries carried this bright red blood to the farthest parts of the body. Then it travelled in the veins back to the heart and began its journey all over again.

This was a tremendous discovery. It was to provide a new and real understanding of the living body but, for the time being, Harvey said very little about it.

By Act of Parliament, the College of Physicians was allowed to dissect the bodies of four criminals a year and, in 1615, Harvey was appointed Lecturer in Surgery for a fee of £40 a year. He was to lecture on Wednesdays and Fridays at ten o'clock until eleven, speaking at first in Latin and then in English.

He planned his work carefully. During the first year, he dealt with ulcers, wounds and broken bones and, in winter, when a dead body would keep longer, he dissected "the inward parts" of a man. In the second year, before a gathering of doctors and privileged visitors, he dissected the trunk; in the third year, the head; in the fourth year, a leg and an arm; in the fifth year, he dealt with the skeleton and the setting of broken bones and in the sixth year, with general surgery. After that, he began the course again.

When Harvey gave his first lecture in April 1616, we know that he had already discovered the circulation of the blood because his notes still exist. This is what he said:

"It is plain from the structure of the heart that the blood is passed continuously through the lungs to the aorta. . . . It is shown that the passage of the blood is from the arteries into the veins, whence it follows that *the movement of the blood is constantly in a circle* and is brought about by the beat of the heart."

In public, Harvey had contradicted the teaching of 1500 years and, curiously enough, there was no immediate outcry. Perhaps he spoke briefly and quietly. The rest of his lectures were brilliant and it only got out gradually that the little doctor had some

"It is finished!"

quaint idea about the blood. The rumour reached a master-printer in Germany who published medical books.

One evening, Harvey laid down his pen and turned to his wife while her favourite parrot (that he was to dissect one day) strutted up and down the arm of her chair:

"It is finished," he said. "After twelve years I have written in full my account of the circulation of the blood."

"And will thou send it now to Master Fitzer at Frankfurt?" asked Mistress Harvey.

"Tomorrow," replied her husband. "He hath begged for it this long time in order to have it printed in time for the great Book Fair. He saith in his letter that it will make a stir in Europe."

The book caused a sensation. Opponents poured ridicule and abuse upon the author. Books were published in Venice, Holland and France to prove him wrong, and in London the attacks were so fierce that, for a time, Harvey believed that he was ruined.

"I have fallen mightily in my practice," he said ruefully. "All the physicians are against me and many persons declare that I am no better than crack-brained!"

However, he soon recovered his spirits and remarked to his wife:

"I shall not answer my enemies. Time will prove me right and, when it does, I need say nothing more."

But his brother-physicians had not forsaken him. In 1629 he was elected Treasurer of the College, and shortly afterwards King Charles I commanded him to travel abroad with the Duke of Lennox.

The doctor was delighted to visit the Continent for the first time since his student days. He was away for a year in France and Spain where he noted that the effects of war and plague were so bad that

"by the way, we could scarce see a dog, crow, kite, raven or any other bird *or anything to dissect* . . ."

After he came home, Harvey was honoured by being made Physician-in-Ordinary to the King at the huge salary of £300 a year and this was later increased to include an apartment at Whitehall and £200 for his food and wine. Charles I became very fond of his little doctor and liked to have his company when travelling and hunting. Naturally, Harvey obtained permission to dissect the bodies of deer in the royal parks and, in Scotland, he was far less interested in His Majesty's political troubles than in animals, birds and the way a chicken develops in the egg.

When Charles left London to prepare for war, Harvey was over sixty but, as the King's doctor, he went with his master. Yet, even when Charles was collecting troops, Harvey rode off to Derby to visit an old friend in order to discuss child-birth and illnesses of women.

In due course, he found himself with the royal army at Edgehill where he was given charge of the King's sons, the Prince of Wales, aged twelve, and the Duke of York who was ten. Prudently, he persuaded the excited boys to accompany him to the shelter of a wide ditch and, while the princes peered through the hedge to see how the battle was going, Harvey took a book out of his pocket and began to read, quite unaware of the gunfire and thundering cavalry no great way off. Suddenly, a cannon-ball whistled through the hedge, ploughing into the ground and spraying the doctor with earth.

At this alarm, Harvey closed his book and led the boys to the rear where he was soon busy with the wounded. An observer wrote afterwards that a certain cavalier was lying on the field among the slain "as a dead person but, brought off by his son, he was recovered by the immortal Dr. Will Harvey who was there under a hedge when the battle was at its height".

After Edgehill, the King made his headquarters at

At Edgehill

Oxford and here Harvey spent the rest of the war, content to be able to continue his work. He was grieved, however, to learn that in London a mob had broken into his house:

"I here give vent to a sigh," he wrote sadly. "Certain persons not only stripped my house of all its furniture but, what is matter of far greater sorrow to me, my enemies took from my museum all those papers and things on which I have spent years of toil."

After the surrender of Oxford, he returned to London. His wife had died, he had no children and his home was destroyed. But his brothers, five of them still alive and all prosperous merchants, welcomed him to their homes and he passed the rest of his life visiting them in turn.

He was particularly fond of his brother Eliab who, for many years, had looked after the doctor's money since he himself had no head for business. At Eliab's house in the City or at his country residence at Roehampton, the now white-haired doctor was happy with his nieces and their children.

As he grew older, he became rather odd in his habits. When gout pained him, he would go up to the flat roof of the house in frosty weather and sit with his feet in a pail of water until they were numb; at meal-times, he would sit himself down and start eating whether or not the company was seated and he insisted upon having a great salt-cellar filled with sugar which he sprinkled on his food—meat, vegetables, everything! Often, he was to be seen walking about the fields, observing insects and small creatures in the grass, all the time combing his white hair with great energy, and then he would go and sit in a cave in the grounds, declaring that he could think better in the dark.

In his eightieth year the little doctor died at Roehampton surrounded by his brothers and their children. His body was taken to the family vault at Hempstead in Essex where, more than two hundred years later, the College of Physicians placed his coffin in a white marble tomb in the church.

Harvey has been called the greatest genius of English medicine, and his discovery has been likened to that of Christopher Columbus. Both men proved that the old ways of thought were wrong, both opened the door to knowledge. Columbus discovered a continent, Harvey laid the foundation of modern medicine.

Prince Rupert

"HE is still a little giddy, though not so much as he has been. Pray tell him when he does ill, for he is good-natured enough—but he does not always think . . ."

Elizabeth, "the Winter Queen", sighed as she paused in the middle of her letter to a friend in England . . . if only Rupert were as steady as his brother Charles-Louis . . . but he had always been a wild boy . . . no wonder his sisters called him Rupert-the-Devil . . . She hoped that he would behave himself in England at the Court of his uncle, Charles I . . .

The widowed Queen need not have worried about seventeen-year-old Rupert. Charles I and the English Court were delighted with the massive young Prince who was so much more lively than his solemn brother. He rode and shot superbly, he was unbeatable at tennis and as interested in drawing and chemistry as in sport.

Rupert enjoyed himself so much that he did not wish to leave and his mother had to command him to return to Holland.

On his last day, as he rode out to hunt with the King, he turned to his uncle and exclaimed:

"Sire, I wish that I might break my neck in the field, so that I would leave my bones in England!"

Back at home, he soon forgot his disappointment

Rupert returns home

when his mother allowed him and his young brother Prince Maurice to join a Dutch regiment. They took part in a daring attack on a Spanish garrison, and in the following year Rupert went to Germany to try to win back his father's estates. He was serving as a colonel-of-horse with the Swedes against the Austrians when he was captured and taken to a castle overlooking the Danube. During a long captivity, his kindly jailer allowed him to paint, to study and to ride out on parole with Boy, a white poodle given him by the Ambassador at Vienna.

Three years passed before his uncle succeeded in persuading the Emperor to set him free.

On Christmas Eve 1641, with Boy scampering ahead, Rupert rode into the courtyard of his mother's house in Holland. He asked for news. Where was Maurice? How were his sisters? Was Charles-Louis in England again?

When he learned that England was on the brink of civil war, he cried to his mother:

"I will leave at once to offer my sword to my uncle."

It was August, however, before Queen Henrietta Maria handed him his commission as Captain-General of the Royal Horse. With Maurice and the white poodle, he reported to the King at Leicester and immediately went to inspect the cavalry.

He was twenty-two and some of the senior commanders looked down their noses at this youngster promoted over their heads. But the Prince had eyes only for his men. He rode down their ranks, a splendid figure in crimson silk with lace at his wrists, raising his plumed hat as they shouted:

"King Charles! King Charles! Hang up the Roundheads!"

Yet, for all their enthusiasm, they did not impress Rupert. He had seen enough of professional soldiers to recognize that these eight hundred young bloods, squires' sons and pink-faced farmers had everything to learn. They were laughably ill-equipped and had little notion of discipline.

As the royal army moved westwards, Rupert worked like a fiend to train the cavalry. Soon, the very name of Rupert began to alarm the Parliamentmen:

"This diabolical cavalier flies with great fury through the counties," they complained, "raising men for the King in the most rigorous way. It is impossible to bridle his fierceness!"

By the time the army approached Shrewsbury, Rupert had increased his command to 3000 well-mounted horsemen who, for the next two years, were to prove themselves the finest cavalry in Europe.

In September, the Earl of Essex, Parliament's general-in-chief, marched from London with a large army. The King withdrew from Worcester and Rupert, commanding the rear, took four hundred horse to discover the enemy's intentions. Resting in a field at Powicke Bridge, he realized from the glint of steel through the hedgerows that a force of cavalry was advancing ahead of the Parliamentary army.

In breeches and shirt, he ran to his horse, shouting to Maurice and the rest to follow. They leapt the hedge and fell upon the unsuspecting Parliament troops as they emerged from a narrow lane. Someone shouted "Wheel about!". The lane became choked with panic-stricken horsemen who broke formation and fled across the fields.

In a few minutes, a thousand men were routed and four hundred killed by a handful of cavaliers without body-armour or pistols.

At Ludlow, the King was overjoyed by his nephew's success:

"Let your Majesty but give the command and we shall take London within a month," cried Rupert.

The King was doubtful but, yielding to his nephew's pleading, he ordered the advance. Meanwhile, Essex hurried up to bar the way and the two armies came face to face at Edgehill in the centre of England.

In the King's camp a fierce argument took place. Lord Lindsey, the elderly commander-in-chief, proposed cautious tactics while Rupert urged a shock attack in the style of the Swedes. The King supported his nephew, whereupon Lindsey threw down his baton angrily:

Powicke Bridge

"If I am to be overruled by a boy, I will die a colonel at the head of my own regiment!" he cried. Rupert had already gone out to his cavalry.

"Ride close, sword in hand, until you break in amongst the enemy. Not until then shall you use your fire-arms," he ordered.

The young cavaliers could hardly contain their excitement. At the word of command, they hurtled down the slope and broke clean through the opposing ranks. Hallooing for joy, leaping hedges and ditches, they hunted the fleeing enemy across country with never a thought for the battle on the slope behind them.

Against orders, the reserve cavalry had followed Rupert, so there was no cover for the King's infantry. In hard fighting, the Royal Standard was lost,

The King's Council

Lindsey was killed and those around the King begged him to fly.

At this critical moment, Rupert returned, having frantically rounded up some of his scattered troopers. The Standard was re-taken and, as darkness came on, the exhausted armies drew apart, both claiming the victory.

Next day, Rupert strode into the King's council of war to urge boldness.

"We are between the enemy and the capital," he said. "Let me ride with three hundred horse and I will be in London and have Parliament dissolved before my Lord Essex has his breath back!"

The King hesitated. Hoping to avoid any more bloodshed, he listened to half a dozen plans. Lord Digby, a tricky, dangerous man, disliked Rupert;

parrots. These pleased Dampier "because they would prate very prettily".

The buccaneers captured a few ships and shared the plunder. Having some money in his sea-chest, Dampier left them, bought a passage to England and reached his brother's farm after an absence of four and a half years.

Dampier writes his journal

In Devonshire he fell in love with Judith, a lady's maid from the Duke of Grafton's household. They were married and, in the spring, Dampier said good-bye to his bride and sailed to Jamaica. He took with him a consignment of saws, axes, hats, stockings, shoes and rum.

On landing, he sold his goods on the quayside and sent the money home to buy a small estate in Dorset. He was about to go back to join Judith there when he fell in with a Mr. Hobby who proposed a short trading voyage.

Never able to resist the chance of "knowledge and experience", Dampier set off with Hobby but, in the first bay they came to, they found a dozen ships lying at anchor. Their own vessel was quickly boarded by a jovial set of ruffians who broached a cask of rum and revealed that they were about to sack the town of Porto Bello.

Hobby's crew immediately deserted to the buccaneers and it was not long before Dampier realized that he must join them or starve.

Porto Bello was captured without much trouble. The buccaneers crept through the woods and surprised the garrison with a sudden dash. When the booty was counted, it came to £40 a man.

A council was held to decide the next step and it was resolved to try their luck across the Isthmus of Panama.

Leaving a party to guard the ships, 330 men set off into the tropical forest, a coloured flag at the head of each company. Dampier was there with two friends, Basil Ringrow and Lionel Wafer, a young chemist who was now the surgeon's mate. Like the rest, they were clad in seamen's jackets, blue waistcoats, wide breeches and black stockings. On their heads they wore red caps and, besides weapons, each man carried several "doughboys"—hard dumplings baked in sea-water. Wafer had his medical chest and Dampier his precious journal that he kept in a piece of bamboo stoppered at either end with wax.

Aided by the Indians, who hated the Spaniards, the buccaneers crossed the Isthmus but, at Panama, they were repulsed with the loss of forty killed and wounded. However, they seized a Spanish ship and made off down the coast in search of easier prey.

At this point quarrels broke out. Captain Coxon, accused of cowardice in the fighting, withdrew in a huff and recrossed the Isthmus with seventy men.

Sawkins, a most valiant man who had made his ruffians observe the Sabbath and give up gambling, became the new leader. When he was killed in a headlong attack on a Spanish fort, Captain Sharp, a smooth-tongued rogue, took command.

Crossing the Isthmus of Panama

There were more raids, another mutiny and a desperate affray at Arica, the silver port of Peru. The buccaneers stormed into the town but they were driven back with heavy losses.

The survivors drew off to an island.

"Rather than serve longer under Captain Sharp, I will desert this crew," cried one. "Who is with me?"

More than forty raised their hands, including Dampier and Wafer. They resolved to cross the Isthmus by a roundabout route.

It was a terrible journey. They had no food, except a little flour, chocolate and sugar. The route lay through dense forest criss-crossed by rivers, so they could hardly make six miles a day.

"We gave out that if any Man faltered on the journey, he must expect to be shot to Death, for we knew that the Spaniards would be after us and one man falling into their hands might be the ruin of us all," wrote Dampier. Soon, their sufferings were greater than their fear of the Spaniards.

Two or three laggards were lost, one man, weighted down by his bag of dollars, was drowned crossing a river and Wafer, having had his kneecap blown off, could only hobble in agony. Fortunately the Indians befriended them and sheltered Wafer in one of their villages with some others who could go no further.

The rest struggled on to the coast and were taken aboard a French privateer.

Before long, the Englishmen were reunited with Coxon and their old companions in a nearby anchorage. They cruised along the Spanish Main, taking prizes, quarrelling and drinking in their usual style until some of the more sober characters decided to make north to Virginia where they could sell their share of the booty without too many questions.

After a spell ashore, Dampier joined the crew of the *Revenge* with Wafer and Ringrow who had turned up none the worse for their adventures. Fresh water was taken aboard but no meat except "shark that was boiled and stewed with vinegar and pepper". Undismayed, the buccaneers rounded the Horn and came to the coast of Peru.

Here they joined a pirate fleet of ten sail and rampaged up and down the coast capturing ships and pillaging towns to their hearts' content.

Between raids Dampier found plenty to interest him:

"The Sea-lion is a large creature about 12 to 14 foot long . . . it hath a broad face with many long Hairs growing about its lips like a Cat. It has a great goggle eye . . . The 9th of May we arrived at this Isle where there is a small Cove or sandy Bay where ships may careen . . . there are Fowls in great multitudes called Boobies but mostly Penguins, a Sea Fowl about as big as a duck and such Feet, but a sharp Bill, feeding on Fish. They do not fly but flutter . . . their Flesh is but ordinary Food but their Eggs are good Meat. There are 4 sorts of Sea-Turtle which I shall now describe . . ."

After a year of raiding, Dampier decided to leave his ship to throw in his lot with Captain Swan of the *Cygnet*.

Swan, a fat blustering man, took Dampier aside and whispered:

"I am resolved to quit buccaneering lest it bring us to the gallows. Wilt thou pilot my ship across the

Pacific that we may resume honest trade in the East Indies?"

Downcast by Ringrow's death and Wafer's transfer to another ship, Dampier agreed to go, though the *Cygnet*'s crew looked even more villainous than his own.

It was a hard voyage with provisions down to a handful of maize daily per man. One sailor, caught stealing food, was given three lashes from every man on board and when, after fifty-two days, the *Cygnet* reached the Philippines, there were three days' rations left and the crew had secretly planned to kill the captain and officers and eat them. Hearing this, Swan remarked to his lean pilot:

"Ah, Mr. Dampier, you would have made them but a poor meal!"

At Mindinao, the Englishmen were so well entertained by a friendly Sultan that Swan spent all his time ashore, growing fatter and more brutal every day. At length, the buccaneers decided to abandon him.

Being unwilling to sail without a doctor, they tricked Mr. Coppinger, the assistant surgeon, into coming aboard. By chance, Dampier happened to be with him. Both were seized and the *Cygnet* put to sea, leaving Swan and thirty-six others stranded on the island.

From the piracy point of view, the voyage was a failure and by the time they reached the Nicobar Islands in the Indian Ocean, the men had become so violent that Dampier decided to escape at all costs.

He obtained a canoe and, with two Englishmen, a Portuguese and four Malays who fitted outriggers to

The escape of Achin

the tiny craft, he set out to cross 150 miles of sea to Achin, an English trading post.

A storm came up so gigantic that even Dampier was terrified:

"I have been in many dangers," he wrote, "but the worst of them was but a Play-game compared with this."

Praying for God's help, he steered night and day, while the others baled for their lives. On the fifth day, they staggered ashore on the island of Sumatra and collapsed from exhaustion and fever. Two of the adventurers died but the rest managed to reach Achin where they were treated kindly by the merchants.

Anyone but Dampier would have accepted their offer of a passage home. Troubled by fever, as thin and ragged as a scarecrow, he still could not bear to leave this part of the world that he knew little about. His boyhood dreams led him on and he took ship with a Captain Weldon to go trading to Indo-China. He made journeys far inland to study strange tribes, became mate to a crew of Moors, sailed to India and the coast of China and back again to the East Indies where he took the post of gunnery officer to an English trading fort.

Finally, he obtained a passage home "and we luffed in for the Downs where we anchored on September the 16th, 1691".

The ex-buccaneer had been away for twelve and a half years and his sole possessions were his journal and a much-tattooed native named Prince Jeoly whom he had befriended in the East Indies when, as a prisoner-of-war, the man was put up for sale. Needing money to reach Devonshire, Dampier had to part with his servant who went on show in London as "The Famous Painted Prince, the Wonder of the Age".

For the next few years, Dampier seems to have lived quietly at home with Judith, earning what he could and putting into order those smudged tattered notes that he had kept in a bamboo tube as he swam rivers, had dried over fires on deserted beaches and had carried inside his shirt through all the tempests, fights and adventures of twelve years round the world.

The story of his travels was published in 1697 with the title *A New Voyage* and, within days, Dampier was famous.

All London wanted to read his book. New editions were printed and the modest author found himself taken up by fashionable people, by scientists, geographers and merchants. His portrait was painted, his advice was requested for voyages and overseas ventures. Everyone wished to meet him; Mr. Pepys of the Navy Board invited him to dinner one evening and John Evelyn noted in his diary:

"I dined with Mr. Pepys, where was Captain Dampier who had been a famous buccaneer, had brought hither the Painted Prince and printed the story of his very strange adventures. He was now going abroad again by the King's encouragement . . . He seemed a more modest man than one would imagine."

"The modest man" was appointed captain of the *Roebuck* with George Fisher as his lieutenant. Their mission was to explore the unknown land of Australia "a country likely to contain gold".

From the start Dampier was unlucky. He had never commanded a ship before, his crew were a surly, timid lot and Fisher, a regular Naval officer, made no secret of his contempt for a captain who had been a low-down pirate.

When they got to sea, Fisher quarrelled violently with the bo'sun and thrashed a midshipman unmercifully. At the first taste of bad weather, he showed pitiful ignorance and cast such doubt upon his captain's skill that he made the crew even more panicky than they would have been.

"The ignorance and obstinacy of some under me occasioned me a great deal of trouble," wrote Dampier in his mild way when he was actually facing a mutiny led by his own lieutenant. There was a scene on deck when Fisher called the captain:

"Old Rogue! Old Dog! Old Cheat!"

Sent to his cabin, he continued to bawl threats until Dampier had him put into irons. He would have to get rid of Fisher.

When they reached Brazil, the lieutenant was taken ashore and lodged in a Portuguese jail until a ship arrived to carry him to England. Unperturbed, Dampier sailed on and on 6th August 1699, dropped anchor in Shark's Bay, Western Australia.

The crew were suffering from scurvy and the ship was showing signs of being unsound, but the land looked attractive and there seemed to be every prospect of success. Parties went ashore but, try as they would, they could find no fresh water and the aborigines, whom Dampier approached with great courage, were murderously unhelpful.

Had he now turned south, Dampier must have made a thorough discovery of Australia seventy years before Captain Cook. As it was, he sailed northwards out of Dampier Bay to search for water along the barren coast.

By this time, the men were almost dying of thirst. Reluctantly, Dampier steered away from the land to Timor where he could obtain water. For several weeks, he "jogged on", exploring the coast of New Guinea, naming capes and islands and recording his

Dampier with the Aborigines

notes on the natives and vegetation of unknown islands.

The *Roebuck*'s timbers were found to be so rotten that it was impossible to return to Australia. The sole hope was that she would last out the voyage home. Dampier nursed her skilfully round the Cape but, in February 1701, she foundered off Ascension Island.

The captain got his men ashore on rafts and they lived on turtles and shellfish until a passing vessel took them off and carried them to England.

At once, Dampier had to face a court-martial. Lieutenant Fisher had returned long since to make his tale good and the Court found Dampier guilty of "Hard and Cruel Usage against Lieutenant Fisher". He was fined all his pay and was declared "not a fit person to be employed as Commander of any of His Majesty's ships".

It was a harsh decision against a captain who had made important discoveries and had managed to control a difficult crew once Fisher was off the ship. Perhaps their Lordships felt that they had been unfair for, within a year, Dampier was given a new command.

War with Spain had broken out and, in 1703, the *London Gazette* announced that Captain Dampier, being about to depart in the *St. George*, "had the honour to kiss the hand of Her Majesty, Queen Anne".

He was given a roving commission and, with Captain Stradling of the *Cinque Ports*, he made for the old buccaneering coast of Peru. Several Spanish vessels were taken but the treasure town of Santa

Maria proved to be too tough a nut to crack. As usual, failure led to quarrels. Stradling went off alone, and after a bitter wrangle with his mate, Alexander Selkirk, left him on the uninhabited island of Juan Fernandez. This brutal act was to supply Defoe with his immortal story of *Robinson Crusoe*.

Meanwhile, Dampier put into a quiet bay to careen his ship. To his dismay, he found that she was as rotten as the old *Roebuck*, for her timbers were "eaten like a honeycomb" and, in places, the carpenter could push his thumb clean through the planks! Repairs were going on when the mate and twenty-one malcontents stole the longboat and sailed away with most of the provisions.

Dampier had plenty of pluck. With a leaky ship and a weakened crew, he ordered a desperate attack upon a Spanish treasure galleon known as the "Manila ship". This failed and thirty-five more of the crew deserted in a captured barque.

With only twenty-eight men left, the tough old captain actually captured the town of Puna, seized a Spanish ship into which he transferred his crew, crossed the Pacific and got back to England in 1707.

Not surprisingly, poor Dampier was now regarded as "an unlucky captain". At fifty-six, he was hard-up and out of a job when Captain Woodes Rogers of Bristol invited him to join a privateering expedition as "Pilot for the South Seas".

The *Duke* and the *Duchess* left the Downs with crews that were mostly "tailors, tinkers, pedlars, fiddlers and haymakers". But Rogers was a breezy, masterful commander. He put down a mutiny and licked these landlubbers so thoroughly into shape that they endured a terrible passage round the Horn, captured a Spanish town with immense booty and 30,000 pieces-of-eight and, wonder of wonders, actually took the "Manila ship", the prize that for so long had drawn every buccaneer to those waters.

But the most famous exploit of the voyage was the rescue at Juan Fernandez. Nearing that lonely island, the men espied:

"a solitary person, running on the beach with a white ensign. He was clothed in a goatskin jacket, breeches and cap, sewed together with thongs of the same."

They hailed him and he gave them directions to land in a strange, stumbling voice and ran along the shore like the wind. It was Alexander Selkirk, who had been marooned by Stradling four years previously. Naturally, Dampier went ashore to examine the castaway's hut and the manner in which he had survived for so long.

In October 1711, the expedition returned home with £170,000 on board. For the first time in his life, Dampier had made a profitable voyage, but a lifetime of hardships had wrecked his health and he did not live to receive his share. The buccaneer who carried a note-book as well as a cutlass and pistol had realized all his boyhood dreams.

Celia Fiennes

IN the 17th century, young gentlemen made the Grand Tour and girls stayed at home. Travel for adventure and knowledge was not for women and there was no such person as a lady-explorer until Mistress Celia Fiennes* set out to visit every county in England.

Celia was brought up in a family, not of Puritan kill-joys, but of sober Dissenters or, as we should say, Nonconformists. Her grandfather was Lord Saye and Sele, nicknamed "Old Subtlety" for his wily opposition to Charles I, and her father was the Colonel Fiennes who surrendered Bristol to Prince Rupert. The entire family supported Parliament and no fewer than eight of Celia's uncles fought against the King.

The Fiennes were moderately rich and very well connected. There were baronets, knights and even an earl in the family and, during her travels, Celia called upon uncles and cousins who were prosperous squires and well-to-do business men in London and the towns. Nor were the Fiennes ruined when Charles II came back. They kept their estates and Colonel Fiennes died unmolested in 1669 when Celia was seven years old and her sister Mary was six.

* Fiennes is pronounced "Fines"

Mistress Fiennes and Celia set out, riding side-saddle

The two little girls grew up at Newton Toney in Wiltshire. Girls of good family hardly ever went to school and Celia and her sister received their first lessons from their mother and afterwards from a tutor.

Celia did not care much for lessons. At the beginning of her Journal, she writes:

"Wiltshire is a fine champion country, pleasant for all sports—Rideing, Hunting, Coursing, Setting and Shooteing",

making it clear that she preferred outdoor sports to spelling! Certainly, the Journal is full of mistakes in grammar, history and geography, but "I speak and write with freedom and easyness" she remarked gaily, as she scribbled away.

When Celia was twenty-two, her sister married Mr. Harrison, a rich merchant, and went to live in London, leaving Celia and her mother in Wiltshire.

Naturally, they missed Mary. The house and the park seemed dull without her and Mrs. Fiennes noticed that Celia appeared to have lost interest even in exercising her horses. She had always liked to be out and about, to watch the wheelwright at work, to help in the brewhouse and harness-room. Now she was listless and bored, forever complaining of headaches and colds. Alarmed lest her daughter should become genuinely ill, Mrs. Fiennes proposed a change of air.

"We will take a journey to view the countryside," she said. "Thomas shall ride with us to be our protector and I have in mind to call upon our relative, Sir William Constantine, and upon Cousin Collier in Dorset."

Mother and daughter set out, riding side-saddle. Thomas and a lady's maid followed, with the spare horses and enough baggage to provide for a change of clothes.

They rode first to Salisbury to see the cathedral and on to the great house at Wilton where Sir Philip Sidney wrote *Arcadia*. Celia, already beginning to brighten, was much amused by some devices in the gardens that sprayed water over unsuspecting visitors:

"about 2 yards off the doore of a Grotto is severall pipes in a line that with a sluce spoutts water up to wett the strangers", she wrote.

In Dorset, the travellers rode along by the sea, took a boat to an island, ate lobsters and shrimps and picked some pretty shells on the shore. Celia's spirits rose with every mile. She watched workers making green vitriol, a chemical used in dyeing and making ink, she discovered how they make cider in Somerset, though she thought it a pity that they carelessly pressed all kinds of apples instead of only the best, and in Devonshire she noticed that the lanes were so narrow that packhorses were used instead of waggons.

Asking the way

"All this knowledge so diverts me," she remarked to her mother, "that I intend to keep a journal throughout all our travels."

This was the first of many journeys that carried Celia all over England. Sometimes, she rode with her mother and, after her death, with one or both of the Filmer girls, daughters of her cousin who lived in Hertfordshire. Often, she travelled by herself, with only a servant and a dog for company.

It was an adventure to travel about England in the 17th century. There were no maps, and signposts were only just coming in. Many parts of the country were practically unknown to anyone outside the district, so that guides had to be hired, almost as if the traveller were in Mexico or the Alps. Even so, it was easy to get lost and Celia became quite cross in Derbyshire where "the common people know not above 2 or 3 mile from their home".

The early journeys were made through the southern and western counties. This was pretty easy country for travelling, though in Gloucestershire and Devon the roads were narrow and bad. Hertfordshire clay was almost impassable in wet weather and near Leicester, "I was near 11 hours going but 25 miles". Worst of all was the liquid mud of Sussex, "which is much in deep blind lanes and up and down steep hills".

But once she had caught the fever for travelling Celia could not stop. As soon as winter was over, preparations were made, horses newly shod, saddle-bags packed and she was away down the road.

Bath, where she bathed and drank the waters, Stonehenge, where she counted the stones and got the number wrong, Oxford, "very cleane and pretty broade", Winchester, whose college was founded by an ancestor of the Fiennes, the Isle of Wight, the New Forest, Portsmouth and Southampton, "almost for-sooke and neglected"—all these and a hundred other places were visited and described during the twelve summers since Mary's wedding.

So far, they had been "little" journeys of perhaps

two hundred or three hundred miles—holidays passed in pleasant, familiar country, a few days with one relative, a week with another, with rides of twenty or thirty miles and many a stop to look at interesting buildings and curious occupations. Longing to go farther afield, Celia set out in May 1697 on her Northern Journey.

With her young cousins, Susannah and Mary, and two reliable servants, she left Amwell in Hertfordshire and rode to Cambridge, passing Audley End, the Earl of Suffolk's house that was so vast that it took a running footman all day to open and shut the windows. Cambridge, she thought, was "mostly old and indifferent" but King's College Chapel "the finest building I have ever heard of". Thence to Peterborough and "fenny" Lincolnshire, pausing to visit Burghley House, near Stamford.

Wealthy men were building new houses on a magnificent scale and Miss Fiennes came through a noble park, past smooth lawns, statues, fountains and a vineyard. She found that "my Lord's bedchamber is furnished very rich, the tapestry all blue silk and rich gold thread . . . there was a blue velvet bed with gold fringes and very richly embroidered". But, although she admired the splendid rooms with their marble floors, painted ceilings and walls, she did not approve of the goddesses and nymphs with no clothes on!

Celia liked things to be clean and modern. Old buildings and picturesque towns bored her and she much preferred stone buildings in the latest "London mode", paved streets, sash windows, and prosperous industries.

Thus Nottingham was always her favourite town—"the neatest I have seen, built of Stone and delicate, large and long Streetes, much like London . . . but buildings finer". The people were busy and prosperous. They drank fine strong ale, cultivated good farmland and had many manufactures. Celia noted brick-making and the weaving of stockings, "a very ingenious art", and, at a glass-blower's, "I spunn some of the glass and saw him maake a Swann presently with coloured glass, he makes Buttons which are very strong and will not breake".

Their inn here was very good, but when they reached Yorkshire, they were charged high prices, though food was cheap enough in the markets—a huge codfish over a yard long cost eightpence and a shoulder of veal ninepence. York itself had "but a meane appearance, the Streets narrow, the houses very low". Only the Minster was a noble building and Celia and her cousins clambered up 262 steps to the top of the tower to see the countryside for thirty miles round with the people below like pygmies.

There was a Mint in York and, with her usual enthusiasm, Celia asked if she could make a coin. She stamped out one half-crown but the men would not tell her the secret of milling the edges of the coins.

The spa at Harrogate was worth a visit for it had four different springs of medicinal waters, one being the Sulphur or Stinking Spa whose smell was so horrid that Celia could not force her horse near the well. Even so, she drank a quart of the stinking water, holding her nose as she did so.

Near Harrogate was St. Mungo's Well, a cold spring much favoured by Roman Catholics. Being a devout Nonconformist did not prevent Celia from plunging in: "you cannot bear the coldness above 2 or 3 minutes, then you come out and walk round the pavement and in again . . . I used my Bath garments and put on flannel when I came out to go into the Bed which is best . . . but some will keep on the wet Garments and let them drye to them and say its more beneficial . . . I dipp'd my head quite under every time and found it eased a great pain I used to have in my head and I was not so apt to catch Cold as much as before."

Continuing to Hull, the ladies failed to find an inn suitable for gentlefolk, there being only two or three "sorry alehouses". Fortunately, as it was getting dark, a Quaker took them in and provided them with good beds, stabling and bread, cheese, bacon and eggs for supper.

From Scarborough, where they saw seventy ships going down the coast with coal for London, they made right across country to Derbyshire, passing through Pontefract that supplied all England with liquorice.

The way became more difficult and the northern miles seemed very long because the old British mile of 2428 yards was still in use in those parts. Derbyshire was "full of steep hills and you see neither hedge nor tree but only low drye stone walls" and when they came to a town, the descent seemed so dangerous that they were obliged to employ guides, one of whom lost Celia's bag containing her night-clothes!

The Duke of Devonshire's bath

But it was fascinating country. There were pot-holes to explore and caves to crawl into on hands and knees until they could stand up in a vast echoing cavern dripping with moisture. In these wilds, they came across Chatsworth, the incredibly lavish home of the Duke of Devonshire where, amid its glories, they saw a modern marvel—"a batheing-room, the walls all blew and white marble and you went down steps into the bath big enough for two people; at the upper end are two Taps to let in one hott, the other cold water . . . the windows are all private glass".

At Buxton, Miss Fiennes was highly indignant to find that the landlady intended them to sleep three in a bed and to put strangers in the same room. However, they came to no harm and were given a warm welcome in the Staffordshire home of Sir Charles Wolseley, an old Cromwell-man married to Celia's aunt. At last, through Warwickshire and the "fine town" of Coventry, to Woburn and St. Albans, the ladies came safely home:

"I returned," wrote Celia, "and all our Company, Blessed be to God, very well without any disaster or trouble in 7 weeks time about 685 miles that we went together." After a tour of Kent, in the autumn, she was able to say with pride, "This year, my journeys have totalled 1045 miles, of which not more than 100 miles were in a coach".

Next year, in 1698, Celia made on horseback a journey that would be remarkable if it were done in a modern motor-car. She rode from London to Norwich, across the Midlands to the Welsh border, through Lancashire and the Lake District into Scotland, eastward to Newcastle and then right through the entire length of England to Land's End and back to London. She called it 'My Great Journey'.

She was now thirty-six, and although she never bothers to describe herself, we may picture her riding side-saddle in a full skirt of hard-wearing serge and a demure, high-necked bodice. Over all, wet or fine, she wore her "dust-coat", a huge dun-coloured cloak that kept out rain and wind, and on her head she wore a big-brimmed hat with a scarf tied over the top and knotted under her chin. There was nothing fashionable about her attire. She was a seasoned traveller and she knew the sensible things to wear that would last for weeks in all weathers and still allow her to appear to be a lady of gentle birth when she arrived at a lordly inn or at some country mansion where she dined at his Lordship's table.

Undoubtedly, she was a bit of a tartar—prim, bossy and sharp-tongued, especially to a landlady who tried to cheat her or to a villager who scratched his head and mumbled he didn't rightly know the way. But she was cheerful and fearless, out to enjoy herself and to discover the facts about her own country. Despite her concern to drink the waters of every spa and healing spring she came to, she was really as strong and sensible as one of her own horses!

This time, her companions were a greyhound and two trustworthy servants. Once, in Cheshire, a couple of suspicious characters followed them and jostled her horse but they made off when some other travellers appeared. Near Scotland it was necessary to hire a guide for protection against robbers, but the heyday of highwaymen had not yet arrived and the greatest danger to travellers was the state of the roads.

Celia might have been drowned when her horse stumbled on a flooded causeway near Ely and her "horse's feete could scarce stand" as she crossed the Sands of Dee. In Norfolk, "the roade lay under water which is very unsafe for strangers to pass, by reason of the holes and quicksands" and her horse fell on the slippery cobbles of Lancaster and threw her when falling into a hole in Cornwall.

On this journey Miss Fiennes showed more interest in the ordinary people. She liked to watch them at work, boiling sea-water for salt, mining coal, tin and lead, making cups and saucers in Staffordshire, spinning outside their houses and "knitting 4 and 5 in a company under the hedges". Her sharp eyes noticed the way they patted up butter at Ipswich into the shape and size of a pint-pot and the method of making soap from the ash of burnt ferns "which they make fine and rowle up in balls and so sell them or use them all the year for washing and scouring and send much up to London".

She could not stand people who were lazy. Ipswich folk, she thought, could prosper if they did not suffer from "pride and sloth"; in North Wales, "the inhabitants go barefoote and barelegg'd, a nasty sort of people", but the Scots were far worse: "I tooke them for people who were sick, seeing 2 or 3 great wenches as tall and bigg as any woman sat hovering between their bed and the chimney-corner, all idle and doing nothing . . . tho' it was nine of the clock!" Prim Miss Fiennes had already ridden seven long miles that morning!

Fortunately, there was plenty to enjoy. She liked the oat clap-bread of Westmorland—"they mix the flour with water, so soft as to rowle it in their hands into a ball and then they have a board made round and something hollow in the middle", the dough was clapped on to this and pressed "as thinn as a paper, placed on an iron plate and baked on the coals just to make it looke yellow and be as crisp and pleasant to eate as anything you can imagine".

In Cornwall, where she celebrated reaching Land's

End by drinking a bottle of beer, she noticed that they had no fuel except furze bushes, not even any wood, but they made the most delicious apple-pie with "clouted cream" on top, though she did not care for the local habit of men, women and children sitting round smoking pipes while she ate.

All kinds of things caught her eye as she rode along: oranges and lemons almost ripe in Derbyshire, the way country-folk in East Anglia hung cakes of cow-dung on the walls to dry for fuel, the custom of yoking oxen with horses to pull carts in the North-east, the inland method of keeping live fish in baskets tied to the river-bank so they could be taken out when needed and cooked fresh.

She saw Holy Thursday processions, coach races at Epsom; she drank an amazing variety of healing waters, and was a keen judge of ale which she preferred to the coffee and chocolate that were becoming fashionable. She liked wine but found that it could only be obtained when she was near to the coast.

Mistress Fiennes made some later journeys, mostly short ones in the home counties, but the peak of her achievements as a traveller was in that fine summer of 1697, "in which I had but 3 dayes of wet, except some refreshing showers sometymes and it was all above 1551 miles—and many of them long miles".

No man of her time, not even Defoe, travelled as far or as thoroughly in England as she. As far as we know, she ceased her journeying when she was about forty. Perhaps she thought it was time to settle down, for she went to live in London, near to her nieces, Mary's daughters. She died at Hackney in 1741 and, judging by her will, made when she was seventy-six, she remained a tough, resolute old lady to the end.

After arranging for her own funeral at Newton Toney, she apologized for the fact that she was not as well-off as formerly and so could not leave very much to her dear nieces. However, there was enough money to carry on a charitable gift of food for poor prisoners, to make gifts to her servants, her doctor and a nephew, and to share out her jewellery, silver, furniture and books.

Strangely enough, although the manuscript of her Journal still exists in the Fiennes' home in Oxfordshire, Celia did not mention it in her will—a coffee-pot, a tea kettle and a nutmeg-box but not the journal of our first woman-explorer.

More about the people in this book

JOHN CABOT (*c.* 1450–99) failed to find the North-West Passage but his discoveries were genuine and he made the first notable voyage in an English ship. His son, SEBASTIAN CABOT (*c.* 1476–1557) seems to have been a map-maker who used his father's name and his own charm to gain credit for voyages that he had never made. His evidence in a case brought by Columbus' relatives showed that he had little real knowledge of North America. However, in his old age he helped to awaken maritime interest in England.

LADY JANE GREY (1537–54) was the daughter of Henry Grey, Marquess of Dorset, later Duke of Suffolk, and of Lady Frances Brandon, whose mother was Henry VIII's sister. Thus Jane's misfortunes arose from her nearness to the throne. Had Northumberland's plot succeeded, she might well have proved to be as tough a character as her cousin Elizabeth, for Jane was highly intelligent, as obstinate as the rest of the Tudors and an enthusiastic Protestant.

The HAWKINS of Plymouth were a remarkable family. John's father made voyages to West Africa and Brazil in Henry VIII's reign, sat in Parliament, founded the business of merchants and ship-builders. His elder son, William, was at sea from time to time but mostly he looked after affairs in Plymouth; his grandson (William III) served with Drake, a cousin. John (1532–95) had one son, Richard, who commanded a ship against the Armada and sailed the *Dainty* into the Pacific in 1593 where he was captured by the Spaniards. After several years in prison, he came home in 1602, was knighted, served in Parliament and as Vice-Admiral of Devon. The *Minion* men who volunteered to be put ashore after the disaster at San Juan were killed by Indians or captured by the Spanish. Some were prisoners in Spain at the time when Hawkins (with Burghley's approval) pretended to turn traitor in order to learn King Philip's plan. His price included the release of his old comrades, and a few survivors did reach their homes at last.

The fame of SIR PHILIP SIDNEY (1554–86) rests upon his gallantry in one small action at Zutphen and upon the extraordinary effect he had upon everyone who knew him. His character was so lovable and his gifts so brilliant that it seemed certain that he would be one of the great figures of the age. The Queen's favour hampered, instead of helping his career. Besides *Arcadia*, he wrote a short book, *Defence of Poesie*, and some marvellous love poems (*Astrophel and Stella*) to Penelope Devereux who married someone else.

WILLIAM HARVEY (1578–1657) is honoured throughout the world as the founder of modern medicine, and a lecture in his honour is still given every year at the Royal College of Physicians. He left his money and an estate to the College. His famous discovery was complete in everything except that he did not realize that blood passes from arteries to veins in tiny channels called capillaries. The microscope was not invented until about the time of his death, and Harvey's simple lens (magnifying glass) did not show the capillaries. In his day there were only three hospitals in England, his own St. Bartholomew's at Smithfield, "Bedlam" for the insane and St. Bartholomew's at Rochester.

JOHN SMITH (1580–1631) was the real founder of Virginia, for the earlier attempts to start a colony by Raleigh and Grenville and by John White failed. Pocahontas went to